Latest of Lee

Robert G. Lee

Le Roi Publishers

Jefferson City, Missouri

CONTENTS

DEITY AND DEATH
AND DISPOSITION

"Christ died for our sins" (I Cor. 15:3)

"Christ . . . suffered for sins, the just for the unjust, that he might bring us to God, being put to death" (I Peter 3:18)

"Christ died for the ungodly" (Romans 5:6)

"Christ died for us (Romans 5:8)

"Christ . . . died for all, that they which live should not henceforth live unto themselves, but unto him who died for them, and rose again." (II Cor. 5:15)

"Christ . . . who did not sin . . . bare our sins in his own body on the tree that we, being dead to sins, should live unto righteousness" (I Peter 2:21-24)

1

The Earl of Rochester, reaching the end of his un-
scrupulus life, said, "Would that I had been a blind beggar or
a foul leper rather than to have lived and forgotten God."

Words of like woe and regret, born of thoughts that are
millstones crushing your spirit, can you speak if, drifting on
insidious currents of worldliness and unbelief, you reject
Christ whose blood is your earliest, latest, and only refuge—
and who will be to you in life like the spring sun putting the
fogs of winter to shame, who will quell your remorse, end
your bankruptcy, blot out the accusing and incriminating
record, alter your night into confident morning, bring back
your souls from the pit and your life from perishing (Job
33:18).

In these words, we meet Christ's

I - DEITY. "Christ"

- Christ, though some, with supercilious pose, seek to discredit Him, is the sum of all wonders — in His person, being Son of man without sin and Son of God with power; in His character, being the only person on earth in whom was no sin; in His life, His biography comprehended in the words, "He went about doing good"; in His death, bearing our sins; in His resurrection, bringing life and ummortality to light (II Timothy 1:10); in His ascension, since which time His name has sounded down the corridors of the centuries like the music of all choirs, visible and invisible, poured forth in one anthem while all years acknowledge His solitary grandeur and crown Him with the glory of all history.

Christ, who, existing coequally and coessentially with God, had glory with God and by God was loved before the foundation of the world (John 1:7).

Christ, Creator of all worlds and all things in all worlds (Heb. 1:2 and Rev. 4:11), revealed Himself to us in an infallible revelation—and became flesh, manifesting God (John 1:14).

Christ, who is God, cannot be reduced by any decision to the plane of a mere man.

Christ, Lamb of God slain—"Worthy to receive power, riches, wisdom, strength, honor, glory, blessing" (Rev. 5:12) — Lamb of supernatural preparation, origin, and sacrifice to produce a supernatural salvation—is the sum total of all things involving the soul's salvation. Christ, coming down from the heights of Deity to the depths of humanity—not in the splendors of His deity but with an infant's palpable and pathetic claim for nurture in a woman's arms and nursing at a woman's breast, making your helpless condition His own nature.

Christ, who, by the blamelessness and beneficence of His life, harkened to the feeblest plea for help, weighed the slightest sigh of grief, measured all degrees of heartache encountered by human hearts, never wearying in healing, comforting, and compassionating sinners, had one purpose—to please God, to bless men.

Christ, solution of all your questions, harbor of all your Christian voyages, has the strong arm that enfranchises slaves—and "if the Son shall make you free, you shall be free indeed" (John 8:36).

Christ, whose character is the ALL of God, eternally and inherently—without cause, beginning, mutation, measure, end—free from the coldness of the moralists and the statuesque iciness of Pharisees, stoops to you, saves you, abides with you through life and death, time and eternity.

Christ, solving the mysteries of redemption according to the legal principles of God's government, is the road from all troubles to tranquillities, from bondage to liberty, from darkness to light, from death to life, from damnation to salvation, from the grave to glory.

Christ—Literature's loftiest ideal, Philosophy's highest personality, Criticism's supremest problem, Theology's fundamental doctrine, Christianity's cardinal necessity—is Hell's dread, Heaven's wonder, the only hope of this head-dizzy, body-weary, mind-tortured, soul-famished, sin-smitten, heart-broken, blood-soaked, tear-drenched, war-scarred, bomb-scared earth.

Christ, who spake as never man spake *(John 7:46)*, possesses and dispenses the wisdom which is indispensable, irreplaceable, and incalculable in its priceless treasurers and inestimable riches.

The supernatural hovered over His cradle, fluttered its wings through all the days and nights of His life, spread its dark and starless mantle over His cross, opened the gates of dawn at His tomb, furnished a chariot of Shekinah-cloud glory for His return to the Father's right hand. Supernaturally great was He in condescension when He was *"made of a woman"*, when, as Milton wrote:

"That glorious form, that Light insufferable,

That far-beaming blaze of majesty,
Wherewith He was wont at Heaven's high council
chamber,
To sit the midst of Tribal unity,
He laid aside, and here with us to be,
Forsook the courts of everlasting Day,
And chose with us a darksome house of clay."

Supernaturally wise was Christ when, adding to His own loneliness by repudiating the fellowship of the schools, He taught — speaking to mind and heart and conscience and will with doctrine that is robed and adorned in a dress of many colors, with words which are seas of unfathomed depths where giants must swim, with words which have their limpid and easy shallows where the feet of little children may wade.

Supernaturally marvelous was Christ in His daily life, which illustrated every doctrine of His heavenly mind—a life which circumstances stained not—a life in which no pulse beat was quickened or footstep hurried by popularity, nor fiber loosened by misfortune, nor purpose found faltering because of antagonism, no sin found, though He *"suffered being tempted"* (*Heb. 2:18*).

Supernaturally helpful was Christ in His miracles of mercy — healing the sick, feeding the hungry, cleansing lepers, freeing the devil-possessed, robbing graves, breaking up funeral processions, restoring deranged minds, breaking the bands of all yokes, setting multitudes free from habits that harm and sorrows that hurt.

Supernaturally glorious Christ was, is, and evermore shall be — whose resources cannot be impoverished by any degree of expenditure, who is always, as we have read, the verity of God's truth, the beauty of God's holiness, the purity of God's nature, the reality of God's love, the surety of God's promise, the majesty of God's power, the authority of God's throne, the pity of God's heart, the repository of God's fulness, the legacy of God's will, the ocean of all

God's full and flowing rivers of grace. All men's metaphors of portrayal exhaust their resources to proclaim His glory and to offer the praise incense worthy the adoration which ages have consecrated to Him. A poet, of long ago, wrote:

> *"Oh! who shall paint Him? Let the sweetest tone*
> *That ever trembled on the harps of heaven*
> *Be discord. Let the enchanting seraphim,*
> *Whose anthem is Eternity, be dumb;*
> *For praise and wonder, adoration, all*
> *Melt into muteness ere they soar to Thee.*
> *The sole Perfection, theme of countless worlds!"*

Note now the

II - DESCENT OF DEITY

Think of the declarations concerning the deity of Jesus. Jesus Himself said: *"I and my Father are one" (John 10:30). "The Father...dwelleth in Me" (John 14:10).*

If Jesus Christ was only a man, very few chapters of the Bible would remain: For the evidence of the Scripture is overwhelmingly strong in declaring and authenticating His Deity. The Bible stars Jesus as God. And there never was a time when He was not God, and God in the same sense He is now God — *"God is blessed forevermore" (II Cor. 11:31).*

Christ's deity ancient HISTORY declares, with pages replete with adoration and worship — insisting that the world should commit itself unreservedly to the worship of Him who came down from the heights of Deity to the depths of humanity.

Thinking of Christ stripping Himself of His robes and roles of glory, Flavel said: *"If the sun had been turned into a wandering atom, if the most glorious angel in heaven had changed into a fly, it had been nothing to the abasement of the Lord of Glory."*

Christ's deity *modern history* declares — though many seek to play His deity down to the level of humanity. Christ was God embodied in human flesh, demonstrated in human life, exemplified in human actions, crystalized in human form.

Christ's deity *Literature* declares — asserting, as a constant purveyer of Christ's deity that Christ is the supreme and superlative fact of all ages.

Christ's deity *Art* declares — asserting, through painting and through sculpture and through music, with all their forms, patterns, imagery and harmony that He is the great unlike, standing unique as the supreme and supernatural One.

Christ's deity *Civilization* declares — giving verdict that He is the central, supreme, superlative fact of the ages.

Christ's deity *Reason* declares — giving thought to the forces, functions, and designs of the universe, Reason declares the necessity for recognition of Christ as infinite Creator.

All men's methods of portrayal exhaust their resources to proclaim the glory of his deity and to offer incense worthy the adoration which ages have consecrated to Him.

Supremely does the Bible — regenerative in power, personal in application, inspired in totality, the miracle Book of diversity in unity — declares in many places that Jesus Christ was very God, the eternal God, the personal and omnipotent Creator God — not only the Son of God, but God the Son. Jesus Christ was not a man who became God, but God who became man. Jesus was not a man-God — an apotheosis, but the God-man, an incarnation.

Jesus the eternal Word was made flesh and dwelt among us — and men beheld his glory, the glory of the only begotten of God. We deal with the very God of very God in the person of the eternal Son who became flesh and walked this earth in a human body.

For the salvation of sinners, he divested himself of the glory He had with God before the world was (John 17:5). Jesus, the very brightness of full-orbed Deity, gathered up His pre-incarnate glory and shrouded it in the purposes or facts of the incarnation.

The mysterious incarnation makes us think of Christ's DESCENT. He came down from the heights of deity to the depths of humanity. Yes — down from the adorations of Heaven to the accusations and abominations of earth. Down from the blessedness of Heaven to the bruises of earth. Down from the commendations and cornations of Heaven to the censures and condemnations of earth. Down from the delights of Heaven to the devilish defamations of earth. Down from the enjoyable excellencies of Heaven to the evil excretions of earth. Down from the favor of the heavenly Father's face to the fury of men's faces. Down from the glory place in Heaven to the gory place called Calvary. Down from the holy hallelujahs of Heaven to the villianous jeers of men on earth. Down from the unspeakable kindness of Heaven to the murderous killing of earth. Down from the love of Heaven to the lying of earth's liars. Down from the majesty of Heaven to the miseries of earth — where he had nowhere to lay His head (Matt. 8:20). Down from notableness of Heaven to the nothingness of earth — where He made himself of no reputation and took upon himself the form of a servant (Phil 2:7). Down from the angelic obedience of Heaven to the reprehensible obduracy of earth. Down from the praises of Heaven to the persecution of earth. Down from the quietness of Heaven to the quarrels of earth. Down from the rejoicing of Heaven to the revilings and raucous rantings of earth. Down from the songs of Heaven to the traitordoms of earth and the tree of Calvary. Down from the unanimity of Heaven to the fierce ululations of earth. Down from the virtues of Heaven to the vice and violence of earth. Down from the worship of angels in Heaven to the wrath of wicked men on earth.

Down from the Xanorphica (stringed instruments of music) in Heaven to the Xerostomia (abnormal dryness of mouth - John 19:28) of the cross. Down from Heaven's yearning of heart to earth's yelping men who were as *dogs which compassed Him about" (Psalms 22:16).* Down from the happy zests of Heaven to the wicked zeal of those who hounded Him to crucifixion.

III - CHRIST'S DEATH. "Christ DIED."

Using the two words — "Christ died" — you reach the most transcendent triumph of human articulation ever known.

Against Christ, the object of priestly hatred, the furies of hell and the hatreds of earth, made cruel and deadly assault — spitting their venom and exhausting their powers of anathema and abuse against Him who claimed to be king — and God.

A King? Then a crown He should have! So *the soldiers platted a crown of thorns and put it on his head" (John 19:2).*

A King? Then some insignia of such a high office he should have and wear! So *"Pilate took Jesus and scourged Him" (John 19:1)* — and they tore His quivering flesh to shreds.

A King? *"Then," said they, "our mouths should so testify."* So *"they spit upon him" (Matt. 27:30),* even in His face (Matt. 26:27).

A King? *"Then," said they, "we should offer Him our hands!"* So they smote Him with their hands (John 19:3) — fulfilling the prophecy of their wickedness expressed in the words, *"I gave my cheeks to them that plucked off the hair" (Isa. 50:6).*

A King? Then a regal robe He should wear. So they, with studied indignity, took His own clothes off Him and *"put on Him a scarlet robe" (Matt. 27:28).*

A King? Then a scepter He should have! So they, in vulgar jest, *"put a reed in His right hand, and they bowed the knee before Him and mocked Him" (Matt. 27:29),* and *"took the reed and smote him on the head " (Matt. 27:30).*

A King? Should they not, therefore, prefer for Him liberty when Governor Pilate at the feast, as was the custom, *"released unto them one prisoner whomsoever they desired" (Mark 15:6)?* No. So they, breathing out slaughter against

Christ, preferred freedom for *"one named Barabbas, who lay bound with them who had made insurrection with him, who had committed murder in the insurrection" (Mark 15:7).*

A King? Then He ought to have a coronation song! So they, with the frenzy of a rabble, cried: *"Away with him! Away with Him! Kill Him!"*

A King? Then He ought to have a royal procession! So, with the carelessness and callousness of mule drivers who load a donkey, they loaded Him down with a heavy wooden cross — and Christ *"bearing His cross went forth into a place called the place of a skull."*

A King? Then He ought to have a throne! So they lifted up that cross of pillowless wood for His death couch — Himself nailed naked thereon (John 19:23).

A King? Then He should have some attendants at His throne. So *"there were two others, malefactors, led with Him to be put to death"* — *"and when they were come to the place, which is called Calvary, there they crucified Him, and the malefactors, one on the right hand, and the other on the left" (Luke 23:33).*

A King? Then, He ought to have a king's chalice and a cupbearer! So *"the soldiers also mocked Him, coming to Him and offering Him vinegar" (Luke 23:36).*

A King? Then His bearing under adverse circumstances should be observed. So, with no pity in their eyes and no love in their hearts, "sitting down they watched Him there" (Matt. 27:36).

A King? Then a bed and a pillow He should have when His work and days are done! But 'twas left with Joseph of Arimathea, *"who himself was Jesus' disciple" (Matt. 27:57),* who, having *"begged the body of Jesus " (Matt. 27:58), "wrapped it in a clean linen cloth, and laid it in his own new tomb" (Matt. 27:59-60),* where marred and scarred with the stigmata of the cross, that body, the bruised and battered minister that carried the holy and redemptive purpose of God, was placed away.

Yes, Christ died — preferring humanity to divinity,

earth to heaven, servitude to sovereignty, Calvary's cross to Heaven's throne.

Christ died — putting away sin by the sacrifice of Himself.

Christ died — being the Mercy Seat for the whole world, yet finding no mercy for Himself.

Christ died — wrapping Himself in the agonies we deserve for our misdoings, receiving the wages of sin which He never earned, that we might have the gift of eternal life, which we never deserved.

Christ died — taking all our sins on Himself, that we, by faith in Him, might stand before God with none of our sins on ourselves.

Christ died — willingly, in love, letting God deal with Him as God must deal with sin, in severe and unrelenting judgment.

Christ died — going into awful gloom that we might enter into glory.

Christ died — making a complete sacrifice, ratifying the covenant of His own precious blood, the procuring cause of our redemption, the assurance of the sinner's access and acceptance.

Christ died — yes. And for the ungodly, for us, for our sins. That places us at the cross. This fact makes us to confess:

> "My sins laid open to the rod
> The back which from the law was free,
> And the eternal Son of God
> Received the stripes once due to me.
>
> "By me the sponge of vinegar and gall
> Was placed upon His tongue,
> And when derision mocked His call,
> I stood that mocking crowd among."

But we must consider now

IV - THE DISPOSITION.

By this, I mean that we must do something with Christ. We live and move before God with our faculties discrowned, our hearts corrupted, our consciences perverted, our intellects enfeebled, our will benumbed, our affections disordered by sin — by sin which, though it looks like a cloud no larger than a man's hand, holds a hurricane in its grasp — by sin which, though it promises happiness, gives testimony by its workings that hell with all its power to damn, cannot add one thing to the foul thing sin is. And we must make some disposition of Christ, our sin-bearer.

Christ Jesus yearns for all to come through Him unto God, who *"is longsuffering to usward, not willing that any should perish, but that all should come to repentance" (II Peter 3:9).*

Christ yearns for regenerate followers who will dare anything for Him, for soldiers who will fight His battles, for lovers and friends who will reproduce His mind and carry on His work — *"always bearing about in the body the dying of the Lord Jesus, that the life also of Jesus might be made manifest in our body, for we who live are always delivered unto death for Jesus' sake, that the life also of Jesus might be made manifest in our mortal flesh" (II Cor. 4:10-11).*

You must make some disposition of Jesus — the embodiment of the infinite love of God. You can no more escape death by taking into your heart one hundred bullets fired from a machine gun, no more than you can cradle an ocean in a thimble.

Once, one turbulent day long ago, Pilate, the Roman Governor, asked the question: *"What then shall I do with Jesus who is called Christ?" (Matt. 27:22).* That question the greatest question in the world — an old question, a new question, every man's question, every woman's question, a question of inexpressibly vast importance — is a personal question, your question, from which there is no escape. As Pilate had to answer that question for himself, so it has to be answered by every man for himself, by every woman for herself.

And you can do only one of two things with Jesus — not one of three, four or five — but one of two. Many times you, no doubt, have heard that simple and serious truth. It needs repetition. You can accept Christ OR reject Christ — crown OR crucify Christ — say Yes OR No to Christ — be for OR against Christ — be friend OR foe to Christ — confess OR deny Christ. *"He that is not with me is against me; and he that gathereth not with me scattereth abroad" (Matt. 12:30) says Jesus.*

What will YOU do with Him — when Christ asks you as a Christian for your love and loyalty, influence, and talents, in His service? Will you for Him forsake the vain things that charm you most? Are you willing to decrease that He may increase, until He fills the whole of your horizon? Are you willing to say good-bye to preoccupation of every kind? Will you serve Him with zeal for Christ's own honor and the conversion of men? Do you have wisdom daily to kindle your little torch at His glowing altar? Will you yield your abilities? Are you willing to go through fire and water, make light of obstacles, laughing at impossibilities, *"ride dauntless up to every Dark Tower"* to have Christ speak well of you? Are you anxious to live from now on, not unto yourself, but unto righteousness and unto Christ, who died for you and rose again?

What will YOU who are not saved, *"whose names are not written in the book of life of the Lamb slain from the foundation of the world" (Rev. 13:8),* do with Christ Jesus? Are you afraid of nothing so much as banishment from God?

Reject Christ — and you stand before the sovereign God of this universe stripped of Christ's protecting power. In that position, the stone you have rejected crushes you. Outside of Christ, God is consuming fire (Deut. 4:24). If you take your place before God without Christ as your Saviour, you stand bare in your own unrighteousness — tainted and dirty with sin, cursed with unbelief. Thus you must take the consequences of God's eternal justice and judgment. Therefore, do the right thing with Him who was evilly assaulted that you might be healed — lacerated that you might be liberated — slain that you might be secured — suffered all the tortures of your condemnation for your justification.

Do the right thing with Jesus — and for the weariest day Christ will be your stay — for the darkest hour, Christ will be your light — for your weakest hour Christ will be your power — for death's assault, Christ will be your ally — or for His sudden coming, Christ will be your welcome.

Make the wrong disposition of Christ and in death you have no assurance — in temptation, no strength — in trouble, no refuge — in sorrow, no comfort — in disaster, no courage — in clamor, no judgment — in guilt, no grace — in sin, no forgiveness — in perplexity, no prompting — in darkness, no light — in storms, no calm — in distress, no deliverance — in ostracism, no friendship — Make the right disposition of Jesus — and, through faith in His name, trusting in the omnipotence of His blood, your victory over sin, the world, the flesh, the devil, and eternal punishment is assured. Pinning your faith to Christ's great sacrifice and nothing else, the sacrifice will evermore speak for you — enabling you to stand before God unafraid and unashamed, faultless and free from every stain — a sinner washed in the blood of the Lamb.

The difference between doing the right thing and the wrong thing with Christ Jesus is the difference between joy and sorrow, between love and hate, between victory and defeat, between a palace and a loathsome prison, between abounding health and wasting disease, between hope and despair, between diamonds and dirt, between the shadow of a great rock in a weary land and the noisome pestilence that wasteth at noonday, between abundant life and cancerous death, between coronation on a throne and hanging on a gallows, between the protection of loving arms and the snare of the archer, between salvation and damnation, between

-17-

heaven and hell.

Christ is God's unspeakable gift — and He may be had for the mere taking by faith. The most famous of bridal gifts was that to Placidia from her devoted prince, as she came from the altar, she walked between a double line of fifty princes, each holding a basin — one of pearls, another of rubies, another of diamonds. As she passed, each was presented with the words, "That you may never want." A gift unspeakably more glorious is presented to the soul at its espousal with Christ. Will you foolishly, and with utter disregard for the eternal welfare of your soul, refuse this gift?

And now — no leering or levity evident — no excuses offered, no cowardice shown, no putting off until "a convenient season," no regard given to cruel criticism, no being almost persuaded, not in self-righteousness, but in repentance, do the right and wise thing with Christ. Then, in redeeming you, Christ will bring you up *"out of an horrible pit, out of the miry clay,"* and set your feet upon a rock, and establish your goings, and put a new song in your mouth, *"even praise unto our God" (Psalms 40).* Then, in guidance, Christ will for you *"exalt every valley, make low every mountain and hill, make straight the crooked, make plain the rough places" (Isaiah 40:4).* Then, forsaking you never, Christ will lead you forth by the right way, that you might go to a city of habitation (Psalms 107:7), *"a city which hath foundations whose maker and builder is God"* (Heb. 11:10). The golden city surpassing all splendors, the glorious city transcending all harmonies, the great city eclipsing all wonders — the eternal city which has love for its law, perfection for its standard, holiness for its song, and the glory of the Lamb for its light.

THE TRIUMPHANT TENSE

"But Mary stood without at the sepulchre weeping: and as she wept, she stooped down, and looked into the sepulchre, and seeth two angels in white sitting, the one at the head, and the other at the feet." (John 20:11-12)

2

If you visit Mohammed's tomb — a tomb adorned with diamonds — you say: "Here is the mortal body of Mohammed." If Mt. Vernon you visit and see the tomb of George Washington, you say: "Here is the dust of George Washington who, when alive, was just, pious, humane, temperate, sincere, dignified, commanding." If to Stratford-on-Avon you travel, and look upon the   grave of Shakespeare, you say: "Here is the dust of Shakespeare, that myriad-minded genius." If to Paris you journey and stand before'that magnificent sarcophagus of gilt and gold, " you say: "Here is all that is left of Napolean's body." If you linger in Westminister Abbey, you say: "Here is the body of Queen Victoria." Or, "Here is the body of Robert Burns." Or, "Here is the dust of once-mighty soldiers and once-influencial statesmen." If to Lexington, Virginia, you go, and stand by the tomb of the sweetest memory of the Southland — say: "Here is the body of that great military genius." If to Northfield you wander and stand by the grave of Dwight L. Moody, the preacher who rocked two continents toward God, you say: "Here is the body of Moody," as you read on his tombstone: "He that doeth the will of God abideth forever." If to Springfield, Illinois you go, and, as you stand before the tomb of the railsplitter of Sangamon, you say: "Here is the remains of that master of men who belongs to the ages — Lincoln, who

> *"Held on through blame and faltered not at praise.*
> *And when he fell in whirlwind, he went down as*
> *when a kingly cedar green with boughs goes down*
> *with a great shout upon the hills, and leaves a*
> *lonesome place against the sky."*

Moreover, if you go to that tiny grave of the little dimpled darling who went away and left you with empty arms and an aching heart, you say: "Here is the baby that once nestled in my arms." If you go, some of you, back to the old country graveyard where snows of many winters have fallen, you stand by some grave, and, looking down, say: "Here is where my mother sleeps." If you go, some of you, to some city vault where slate roofs and marble slabs shelter your dead, you say: "Here is the body of my beloved."

On May 1st, 1932, two million people in closely packed ranks passed by Lenin's tomb in Moscow, a day-long parade. And everyone in that vast throng whether he spoke it by word of mouth or not, had to acknowledge: "Here is the body of Lenin."

But if all the millions of all the ages could be brought to life again, and could form a procession and march by the tomb of Joseph of Arimathea, not one could truthfully say: "Here *is* the body of Jesus." All of them, young and old, black and white, red and yellow, rich and poor, of low estate and high estate, could say: "Come see the place where the Lord *lay*." For when you walk into Joseph's garden, you walk off the *present* tense into and upon a glorious *past* tense. There you can assuredly say that His thorn-torn head *lay* — not *lies* — here. You can say: His scourge-cut back *rested* — not *rests* — here. His nail-pierced hands *were* — not *are* — folded here. His fist-beaten face *was* — not *is* — shrouded here. His compassionate eyes *slept* — not *sleep* — here. Here he *was* — not *is*. Mary saw *"two angels in white sitting the one at the head, the other at the foot, where the body of Jesus HAD lain." "Come see the place where the Lord lay"* (*Matt. 28:6*).

Why are most of our tombs dear to human hearts and sweet in human memories? Why, on some days, do I see people going their way to our cemeteries? Because there, "by the flow of an inland river," sleeps in a grave one whose voice was once the music of a home. Why do I see when I go occasionally to cemeteries, somebody here and group of people there by a great tomb and there by a lowly grave placing flowers? Because there, where they place these tributes are some "asleep under the sod and the dew waiting the judgment day," whose eyes, now closed, once held the light of love. Why is every plat "where the blades of the grave grass quiver," where "asleep are the ranks of the dead," a sacred plot? Because of what they now contain, because of what they now have and now hold till "the "trumpet of the Lord shall sound."

I go to the tomb of B.H. Carroll in Texas. I stand with head covered. Why? Because I stand by the grave of that theological juggernaut who left a trail of glory across a wide state.

I stand near the slab that marks the last resting place of Copernicus who gave the name to the system, who was called the mover of the earth and the establisher of the heavens, who asked to have written on his monument in the venerable church at Thun these words:

"I crave not the favor which Paul received, nor the grace wherewith thou didst pardon Peter; I only pray for that which thou didst bestow upon the thief upon the Cross."

And, as there I stand, I say: "Here is the testimony that Copernicus *is* dead."

I stand on the deck of a ship where Judson was buried. And my heart is moved. Why? Because there, somewhere down in the far-reaching, rolling waves, is the hero of many conquests.

I stand by the humble grave in a Virginia cemetery. And my eye is moist with tears while the sunshine of gratitude floods my heart. Why? Because that underneath the sod rests the bones of one of the greatest preachers of our Southland — John Broadus.

So it is with the burial place of father — whether it be a great marble vault or a spot of lowly soil in some obscure village. So it is with the grave of mother, whether she was placed there years ago or only yesterday. So it is with the grave of the little baby, whether the babe was buried in a corner of a country graveyard or marked with a tiny stone in the shadow of great tombs in a city's "city of the dead." So it is with the grave of the neighbor who shared generously of everything he had —except his troubles. So it is with the grave of the lover for whom some heart is still "just a-wearying." So it is with the friend who, when walking the dusty ways of earth with us, lost money but never lost faith in God. So it is with nearly all graves, "from Greenland's icy mountains to India's coral strand." The entombed dust and bones of kindred and friends and loved ones "hallows the place of their entombment." All these graves and tombs are valued because of what they contain, what they now have and now hold. And there is only one tomb that has imperishable glory. It is the tomb of Joseph of Arimathea "where never man before was laid" till therein was placed the body of Jesus, marred and scarred with the stigmata of the Cross, where for the first time in thirty-three years the cruel world left Him alone.

"Now there stood by the cross of Jesus his mother, and His mother's sister, Mary, the wife of Cleophas, and Mary Magdalene" (John 19:25).

"I AM he that liveth, and WAS dead; and, I AM alive forevermore. Amen, and have the keys of hell and of death." (Rev. 1:18).

"Until the day in which he was taken up, after that he through the Holy Ghost had given commandments unto the apostles whom he had chosen; to whom also he showed himself alive after his passion by many infallible proofs, being seen of them forty days and speaking of the things pertaining to the kingdom of God." (Acts 1:2-3).

We rejoice in the triumphant tense of this Triumph of Scripture.

- The triumphant tense justifies to the literal bodily resurrection of the Lord Jesus Christ as the distinguishing mark of Christianity. This sets it apart from all the man-made religions of the world. False religious must stop at the tomb. Christianity takes us to the throne.

The founders of Brahmanism died and are dead. The founders of Hinduism died and are dead. Buddha died and is dead. Lao tsze, founder of Taoism, died and is dead. Confucius died and is dead. Zoroaster died and is dead. The founders of Shintoism died and are dead. Mohammed died and is dead. Mary-Baker-Glover-Patterson-Eddy-Frye died and is dead. The Fox sisters of Spiritism fame died and are dead. "Pastor" Charles Tate Russell died and is dead. Joseph Smith of Mormonism died and is dead. Madame Helena Petrova Blavatsky died, and is dead. Bahaullah, founder of the Bahai movement, died and is dead.

Go to the tombs of Buddha, Lao-tsze, Confucius, Zoroaster, Mohammed, and the other founders of false religions. The bodies of these leaders lie mouldering in the dust.

Go to the tomb of Jesus Christ. Men and angels shout,

"HE IS NOT HERE: FOR HE IS RISEN: COME, SEE THE PLACE WHERE THE LORD LAY!"

Blessed thought! Death cannot keep his prey! The One who was dead is no longer there. He is no longer dead. He is alive.

The whole earth is a cemetery. The sea is a tomb. The disintegrated bodies of millions have been swallowed up. But it will not always be so. At the shout of the Lord of Glory the dead will stand upon their feet. The righteous will be raised for their glorification, The unrighteous will be raised later for their damnation.

Our Lord said, *"I am the resurrection."* At His command this old earth emerged from its watery grave. At His command the saints will be raptured. At His command Israel will be nationally resurrected. At His command this earth will give up its dead, be renovated by fire — purified, made perfect. It will become the seat of the throne of the living God.

Death fleas at His presence. He touched the bier of a young man *"And he that was dead sat, and began to speak"* (Luke 7:15). *"Maid, arise. And her spirit came again, and she arose straightway"* (Luke 8:54-55). He stood before the disintegrating body of Lazarus *"and cried with a loud voice, come forth. And he that was dead came forth"* (John 11:43-44).

He embraces the lost son from the vine-yard with his melodorous garments and shouts, *"This my son was dead, and is alive again" (Luke 15:24).*

John, the beloved, trembles in His presence. He lays His right hand upon him and says, *"Fear not....I am he that liveth and was dead; and behold, I am alive forevermore. Amen; and have the keys of hell and death"(Rev. 1:17-18).*

What is it that distinguishes Christianity from all man-made religions? It is the resurrection of Jesus Christ. Whatever He touches is transformed whether it be individuals or nations. Accept the miracle of the literal bodily resurrection of Jesus Christ, and all other miracles are easily possible.

All the pages of history contain no event more wonderfully interesting than the most tremendous and the most momentous fact of history — the resurrection of Jesus. His resurrection is the foundation and pivotal point of Christianity. His resurrection — the greatest evidence of Christianity, the greatest exhibition of God's power, the greatest truth of the gospel, the greatest reality of faith, the greatest assurance of coming glory, the greatest incentive to holiness — is marked with the fullest credibility. His resurrection — a fact thrillingly touching the human heart — a truth powerfully influencing human character and human destiny — a fact mentioned directly more than one hundred times in the New Testament — is as fully attested as any other historical fact, remote or recent. The resurrection of Jesus — the whole alphabet of human hope, the certificate of our Lord's mission from heaven, the heart of the gospel in all ages — completed Christ's subsitutionary work on the cross.

It was evidence that God accepted the sinless Substitute. Without Christ's resurrection, His crucifixion and death would have been in vain. These two fundamental facts cannot be separated. Christ's cross, purposed from all eternity, prophesied through ages, peered into by angels, found its complement in the empty tomb where Jesus wrestled from Death's brow his black diadem — shivered at a single blow Death's empire of skulls and skeletons, changed humanity's bleak winter into flowery summer, "brought life and immortality to light."

Accept the literal bodily resurrection of Jesus Christ as a fact and you will never doubt that He caused the earth to emerge from its watery grave, that He preserved Noah and his family in the ark, that He overthrew the tower of Babel; that He opened the Red Sea for the Israelites; that He held back the swelling tide of the Jordan; that He locked and unlocked the heavens; that He preserved the witness in the fiery furnace; that He padlocked the jaws of the lions; that

He fed the multitudes, stilled the waves, walked on the waters, read the thoughts of the hearts of men, gave the blind their sight, the deaf their hearing, the mad their reason — He healed the sick — He raised the dead. He lived before He was born. He lived after He died. He always was. He is. He always will be. He is the eternal God. The Alpha and the Omega. The Beginning and the Ending. Best of all He is the Resurrection and the Life. None else can make or fulfill this claim. Because He lives, we shall live. If He comes today, we will escape death. But should He tarry until this earthly tabernacle be dissolved, it is comforting to know that *HE COMES FIRST TO BREAK UP OUR TOMB — THEN TO SET UP HIS THRONE.*

How we rejoice in the truth which John expresses:

"Beloved, now are we the sons of God, and it doth not yet appear what we shall be: but we know that, when he shall appear, we shall be like him for we shall see him as he is" (I John 3:2)

So, listen! *"If thou shalt confess with thy mouth the Lord Jesus, and shalt believe in thine heart that God hath raised him from the dead, thou shalt be saved. For with the heart man believeth unto righteousness; and with the mouth confession is made unto salvation" (Romans 10:9-10).*

Be not hard to convince.

Be not slow of heart to believe.

Be not slow of faith.

Be not foolish of mind.

Let not your heart be so set upon this world that you have no eyes or ears for the world to come.

Come to Christ!

Christ your Physician...you shall have health.

Christ your Bread...you shall never hunger.

Christ your Light...you shall not walk in darkness.

Christ your Joy...you shall have comfort in sorrow.

Christ your Righteousness...you shall have no condemnation.

Christ, your Acquittal — you shall have no sentence. Look unto Him on the cross crucified for your sins. Look unto Him risen from the dead for your justification. I call you to accept this saving Christ — and to accept Him now. You will gain nothing by further delay. Today is the Tomorrow you talked about yesterday. You said, "Tomorrow I will confess Christ." Do it NOW! Tomorrow, being saved, I will join the church. Do it NOW! you said: "Tomorrow, I will let the world know that I am not ashamed nor afraid to accept Him before the world." Do that NOW!

MAN HONORED OF GOD

TEXT:

"If any man serve me, let him follow me; and where I am, there shall also my servant be: if any man serve me, him will my Father honor" (John 12:26).

I would ask you — PLEASE — to pitch your mental tents upon and gather the meditations of your hearts around the words — PORTION, PERSON, PREACHER, PROMISE, PEOPLE, PERFORMANCE, PLIGHT, PERPETUITY, PREFERENCE.

So consider the

I - PORTION

That means a portion, a section, a part of the Bible — as John 12 is. The Bible, greatest book of all ages, has traveled more highways, walked more bypaths, knocked at more doors, and has spoken to more people in their mother tongue than any book the world has ever had, can ever have, will ever have.

The Bible, supernatural in origin, divine in authorship, human in penmanship, infinite in scope, is universal in interest, infallible in authority, inestimable in value, inerrant in all statements, inexhaustible in adequacy, secure in its guidance, regenerative in power, personal in application, inspired in totality — the miracle Book of diversity in unity, of harmony in infinite complexity.

This portion of the Bible sets forth a

II - PERSON

That Person is Jesus Christ — Son of Man without sin, Son of God with power. This One is He whom God hath "*set at His own right hand in the heavenly places, far above all principality, and power and might and dominion and every name that is named, not only in this world, but in that which is to come.*" (*Ephesians 1:20-21*).

This wonderful Person, whom God has highly exalted and has given Him a name which is above every name (Phil. 2:9) is the theme of the Bible.

Yes. Jesus, Son of Man and Son of God. Jesus, as much Son of man as though He were not Son of God, just as much Son of God as though He were not Son of man.

God and man in one PERSON.

As man, he got tired; as God He said, "*Come unto me, all ye that labor and are heavy laden, and I will give you rest*" (*Matt. 11:28*).

As man, He got hungry; as God He fed thousands with a lad's lunch (John 6:9).

As man, He got thirsty; as God He gave living water (John 4:10).

As man, He prayed; as God, He made, in praying, no confession of sin.

As man, He was tempted in all points like as we are; as God, He was without sin, baffling His enemies with the question, "*Who convinceth me of sin?*" (*John 8:46*).

As man, He slept; as God, He arose from sleep and

stilled the raging tempest.

As man, He sorrowed over separation from friends; as God, He promised never to leave them comfortless (John 14:18).

As man, He accepted a village girl's invitation to her wedding; as God, He there changed water into wine.

As man, He was despised of men; as God, *"all the angels of God worship Him" (Heb. 1:6).*

As man, He got lonely; as God, He said *"The Father hath not left me alone" (John 9:19).* 𝄢-29

As man, He longed for human companionship and sympathy; as God, He *"trod the wine-press alone" (Isa. 63:3).*

As man, He wept at Lazarus' grave; as God, He raised Lazarus from the dead.

As man, He grew in wisdom and stature; as God, He *"upholdeth all things by the word of His power" (Heb. 1:3).*

Jesus — "the same yesterday, today, and forever" — is today Heaven's Bread for earth's hunger, Heaven's water for earth's thirst, Heaven's light for earth's darkness, Heaven's GRACE for earth's guilt, Heaven's LOVE for earth's hate, Heaven's WISDOM for earth's folly, Heaven's FORGIVENESS for earth's sins, Heaven's GLORY for earth's shame, Heaven's BEAUTY for earth's ugliness, Heaven's HEALTH for earth's sickness, Heaven's PEACE for earth's strife, Heaven's justification for earth's condemnation. Heaven's SALVATION for earth's damnation.

> *"O, who can paint him? Let the sweetest note that ever trembled on the harps of heaven be discord. Let the enchanting seraphim whose anthem is eternity, be dumb. For praise and wonder, adoration, all melt into muteness ere they soar to Thee, The sole Perfection, Theme of countless worlds."*

There never was anyone like Jesus *before* Jesus. There never has been one like Jesus *since* Jesus. There never will be another like Jesus — before all, in all, all in all.

Now, let us think of this pre-existent Jesus Christ as the powerful

III - PREACHER.

What a teacher this divine preacher was!

The religious authorities wanted Him taken and stopped, and sent to arrest Him on one occasion. And the Scriptures give this account of the event:

> *"Then came the officers to the chief priests and Pharisees; and they said unto them, Why have ye not brought him? The officers answered, Never man spake like this man"* (John 7:45-46).

As a teacher, Jesus stands out above all teachers as a great palm tree in a desert of mediocrity, as a deep and crystally clear river amid shallow and babbling brooks, in reach, as a rifle is above a popgun in power, as a 1000-bulb chandelier is above a cluster of feeble and flickering candles in brilliance.

Say it again! "Never man spake like this man!"

What a chasm-wide and mountain-high difference in the teachings of the greatest philosophers and teaching of Jesus! Put down on one hand the teachings of Sophocles, Pericles, Demosthenes, Socrates, Plato, Aurelius, Confucious, and Aristotle. The difference in their teaching and the teaching of Jesus, who was not stamped with the imprint of the schools and exhibited no diploma from the Sanhedrin, is the difference in speculation and revelation, the difference between inquiry and declaration, the difference between surmise and certainty, the difference between groping and guidance, the difference between perplexity and prompting, the difference between lantern light and sunlight, the difference between weakness and power, the difference between the parrot's raucous squawking and the meadow lark's sweet lyric — yes, the difference in man's little teacup mind and God's oceanic mind.

In boldness of conception, in grandeur of character, in sublimity of purpose, in originality of mind, in valiant propagandism, Jesus' teachings claim the sovereignty of the world.

Today, when the air is troubled with doubts, thick with negatives that have no mission and no adventure and no beneficent audacities, we need to examine the teachings of Jesus — teachings which spurned the established boundaries of His day, leap across conventional gulfs and deep chasms which yawn between race and race, class and mass, sex and sex, sects and sects.

Potently paradoxical is Jesus in His teaching. He taught that men are to live by dying, to win by losing, to hold on by letting go, to get up by getting down, to become rich by becoming poor, to find our lives by losing our lives.

Tragedy when men have no ears to hear His teachings and wills to do His teachings.

Now, give thought to the truth that this preacher-teacher of power and wisdom makes a precious

IV - PROMISE

"If any man serve me, him will my Father honor" (John 12:26). This promise weighs sixteen ounces to the pound on God's scales of truth, *"for it is impossible for God to lie"* (Heb. 6:18). Just as it is impossible for God to repent for sinners or to accept Jesus Christ as Saviour for sinners, just so *"if man serve Me him (that man) will my Father honor."* This promise is the promise of truth. For *"it is impossible for God to lie."*

> *"Every good gift and every perfect gift is from above, and cometh down from the father of lights, with whom is no variableness, neither shadow of turning"* (James 1:17).

THINK of some precious promises Jesus made:

> *"Him that cometh to me, I will in no wise cast out"* (John 6:37).

-35-

This is His promise to the sinfully unsaved.

"Come unto me, all ye that labour, and are heavy laden, and I will give you rest. Take my yoke upon you and learn of me; for I am meek and lowly in heart: and ye shall find rest unto your souls" (John 11:28-29).

This He speaks to all who grow weary in work, in bearing life's burdens, in fighting life's battles.

"I will not leave you comfortless" (John 14:18).
Thus He speaks to the sorrowing and broken hearted.

"Peace I leave with you, my peace I give unto you: not as the world giveth, give I unto you. Let not your heart be troubled, neither let it be afraid" (John 14:27).

"If ye abide in me, and my words abide in you, ye shall ask what ye will, and it shall be done unto you" (John 15:7).

"I am with you always — even unto the end of the world" (Matt. 28:20).

The apostle Peter speaks of the promises of God:

"There are given unto us exceeding great and precious promises" (II Peter 1:4).

All the promises Jesus has spoken will never be broken. Abraham *"being fully persuaded that what He had promised, He was able also to perform " (Romans 4:21) —* rejoiced in God's promise.

"Let us hold fast the profession of our faith without wavering; (for he is faith that promised;)" (Hebrews 10:23).

"Through faith also Sara herself received strength to conceive seed, and was delivered of a child

when she was past age, because she judged him faithful who had promised" (Hebrews 11:11).

"And this is the promise that he hath promised us, even eternal life" (I John 1:25).

In his prayer at the dedication of the Temple, King Solomon said:

"Blessed be the Lord, that hath given rest to his people Israel, according to all that he promised: there hath not failed one word of all his good promise, which he promised by the hand of Moses His servant" (I Kings 8:56).

But I wonder if any promise is more encouraging to help us face life's perilous situations and to fight life's battles than is the promise made in John 12:26?

Take note that this precious promise in John 12:26 includes all

V - PEOPLE

"If ANY man"

This includes people of all races, all colors, all creeds — and of all climes.

This promise is not to the rich to the exclusion of the poor; nor to the poor to the exclusion of the rich, not to the educated to the exclusion of the uneducated, nor to the uneducated to the exclusion of the educated, not to members of the black race to the exclusion of members of the white race, nor to the members of the white race to the exclusion of the black race. Not to folks in Europe to the exclusion of folks in America, not the high-ups to the exclusion of the low-downs nor the low-downs to the exclusion of higher-ups. But if *any man.* Now "ANY" means "WHOSOEVER."

"And the Spirit and the bride say Come. And let him that heareth say, Come. And let him that is

athirst come. And whosoever will, let him take the water of life freely" (Rev. 22:17).

How embracing is the word "ANY" — meaning *whosoever.* It takes you in, it takes me in, it takes teachers in, it takes pupils in. There is many a "whosoever" in the Bible.

There is a "whosoever" of JUDGMENT. "But he that troubleth you shall bear his judgment, whosoever he be" (Gal. 5:10).

"God so loved the world, that whosoever believeth in him....." (John 3:16).

"Whosoever was not found written in the book of life was cast out into the lake of fire" (Rev. 20:15). "Whosoever there includes those who did not come to God while He waited, in grace to save. If they had recognized in the "whosoever" of John 3:16, they would not be found in the "whosoever" of Revelation 20:15.

"ANY" means all, the old, all the young, all the rich, all the poor, all the high, all the low. It includes all the people in the whole wide world, all the faculties in all our schools, all the pupils in all our schools, all the doctors and patients in the hospitals.

"Whosoever" of confession and denial of Jesus.

"Whosoever therefore shall confess me before men, him will I confess also before my Father which is in heaven. But whosoever shall deny me before men, him will I also deny before my Father which is in heaven" (Matt. 10:32-33).

Consider this important word and reality. That word is "SERVE". The reality is SERVICE. That means

VI - PERFORMANCE

The dictionary defines "SERVE" as meaning "to work for," "perform duties for," "Yield obedience to."

So we can really say: "IF ANY man work for me OR

performs duties for me OR yields obedience to me that man will my Father honor. This means more than mere words. This means living in DEEDS. Not *dreaming* but *doing*. Doers of God's commandments we will be — not hearers only. Not WORDS but WORKS.

In the New Testament we read of Dorcas. Every one in the little town of Lydda and Joppa knew Dorcas. She was dressmaker to the poor. She had fitted coats, dresses and baby clothes for years. Of this good woman we read: *"Dorcas was a woman full of good works and almsdeeds which she DID"* (Acts 9:36).

It was not what Dr. Frank Gunsalus of Chicago did for himself but for others, even multitudes, in Chicago, as he preached, tortured with pain and disease he never mentioned to the people.

It was not what Robert Louis Stephenson did for himself, but for others when he wrote immortal books — writing when every hour he was wracked by painful coughing and weakened every week by hemorrhages.

It was not what William Carey did for himself that made him great but what he did for others when it took him five years to win his first convert in India — while and when his little son died and his wife became seriously ill, with all his money gone and the people afraid of him.

Judson — in Burma — lived not for himself but for others. His child died. His wife lost her health. He was put in jail for eleven months in irons amid one hundred degree heat.

Though, in serving Christ, you may never become famous or win the plaudits of the world, you can have part in the lives who do become famous and walk in the flood lights of publicity and have plaudits of multitudes.

For EXAMPLE: Miss Sullivan is not often remembered in relation to Miss Helen Keller, but it was she who directed Helen into a glorious life of achievements.

All lovers of the game of baseball know of Babe Ruth. Listen to what he said of the service of an aged minister

-39-

whose name only a few know: "Most of the people who have really counted in my life were not famous. Nobody ever heard of them — except those who knew and loved them, I knew an old minister once. His hair was white. His face shone. I have written my name on thousands of baseballs in my life. The old minister wrote his on a few simple hearts. How I envy him! He was not trying to please himself. Fame never came to him. I am listed as a famous home-runner. Yet beside that obscure minister, who was so good and so wise, I never got to first base."

> "The world may sound no trumpets, ring no bells,
>> The Book of Life the shining record tells."
>> A child's kiss set on thy sighing lips,
>> Shall make thee glad,
>> A sick one nursed by thee,
>> Shall give thee health;
>> A poor one helped by thee
>> shall make thee rich.
>> Thy love shall chant its own beautitudes--
>> After its own life's working,
>> Thou shalt be served thyself
>> By every sense of service which thou renderest."

Jesus said: "But he that is greatest among you, let him be your servant" (Matt. 23:11).

"And whosoever of you will be the chiefest, shall be the servant of all" (Mark 10:44).

Living as one who serves, we can avoid selfishness, which is the abnormality of life.

> "O the bitter shame and sorrow
> That a time could ever be

When I let the Saviour's pity
Plead in vain, and proudly answered,
    'All of self, and none of Thee!"

"*Day by day His tender mercy,*
Healing, helping, full and free,
Sweet and strong, and, ah, so patient
Brought me lower, while I whispered
    'Less of self, and more of Thee!'

"*Higher than the highest heaven*
Deeper than the deepest sea,
Lord, Thy love at last hath conquered,
Grant me now my supplication --
    'None of self, and all of Thee!'

Think now as to the

VII - PERPETUITY

Perpetuity means "endless duration." This promise is not for one day but for all days, not for one year but for all years; not for one century, for all centuries. It is not as a vapour that appeareth for a little while and then vanisheth, not as a river that goes dry in time of drouth, not as a well that gives water for a little while and then is a well without water — where people let down empty buckets and grow weary with drawing nothing up. This promise is for ALL days, and ALL the years. It was true of all the years that have gone forever into the Tomb of Time. It will be true of any and all years that will yet come from the Tomb of Time.

The laws of gravitation might cease to function or the sun withhold its light, but this promise will never fail.

We are not foolish to think that this promise comes to you when the whole world you must live in is in a

VIII - PLIGHT.

A kind of madness has fallen upon all nations. The

world seems to be undergoing the frightful process of self-burial. In the world Science has drawn fangs from nearly all the killer diseases, but that same Science has placed the total annihilation of the race within the range of easy possibliity — today tyrannical dictators arrange firing squads with no more sense of horror than children building play houses. A defiant and devilish dementia dominates millions in a world of diminishing average intelligence.

Today, this world has a fretful fever worse than that of Peter's wife's mother, a foul leprosy worse than that of Naaman, the Syrian; a blindness more tragic than that of Bartimaeus; an impotency worse than that of the man at the pool of Bethesda, and an insanity worse than that of the wild man of Gadara.

Our court dockets are crowded. Our jails are full of drunks. Our streets are roamed by women who are members of the scarlet sisterhood like unto that headed by Rahab, the harlot. Freedom's speech is being turned into the serpent's hiss and God into marble or pronounced dead by some intellectual abnormals.

Dr. J.B. Lawrence once wrote: "Evil forces work silently within our ranks to undermine or destroy the foundations of our life. There is Materialism — the destroyer of spiritual values. There is Atheism — the destroyer of faith. There is Radicalism — the destroyer of brotherhood. There is Fear — the destroyer of peace. There is Liberalism — the destroyer of sacred tradition. There is Lawlessness — the destroyer of civic order. There is Paganism — the destroyer of Christianity."

Professor Clark said: "From all I can see now, humanism and Communistic hatred of Christianity will be the prevailing philosophy of the coming generation."

I have said these things to say that you must show a

IX - PREFERENCE.

Men must accept or refuse this promise as applicable to their own lives.

The promises of the world are before you. This promise of Jesus is before you. You can choose. Which will your choice be? Joshua 24:15: *"Choose you this day whom you will serve." "No man can serve two masters"* (Matt. 6:24). *"Ye cannot serve God and mammon"* (Luke 16:13).

You can choose to be a friend of God — as was Abraham. *"Abraham was called the friend of God"* (James 2:23).

You can choose to be a friend of God OR an enemy of God. *"....know ye not that the friendship of the world is enmity with God? Whosoever therefore will be a friend of the world is the enemy of God"* (James 4:4).

What is your preference? You can choose the broad way that leads to destruction OR the narrow way that leads to life everlasting. Which do you prefer?

You can choose to be a wild Absalom — a wolf in angel's clothing OR a Joseph, the noblest man mentioned in the Bible in the Book of Genesis — proving that a good man, wherever he goes, cannot put himself beyond God's care. What is your preference?

> *"For the Lord God is a sun and shield:*
> *the Lord will give grace and glory:*
> *No good thing will he withhold from them*
> *that walk uprightly"* (Psalms 84:11).

Now — what is your preference? You can choose to be like Abner who died as the fool dieth, OR like Caleb who followed the Lord fully (Numbers 14:24).

What is your preference? As a woman you choose to be a Jezebel or Delilah to wreck havoc on the good OR a Ruth to utter immortal words or a Mary of Bethany to serve Christ. What is your preference?

You can choose to be sordid and sinful or to keep your self unspotted in a crooked and perverse and adulterous generation. What is your preference? You can choose to be a greedy Midas of avarice or a generous Barnabas. What is your preference?

You can count Christ out — shut Him out of your life — OR you can count Him in, giving Him reign over yourself. But whoever shuts Christ out is acting as those who would take heat out of fire, melody out of music, mind out of metaphysics, numbers out of mathmatics, fact out of history, fiction out of literature, brains out of the skull and expecting intelligence, blood out of the body and expecting health. You can choose to make your life a Nero of evil or a Gladstone of righteousness — concerning whom this was said:

> "*In Christ his mighty intellect found anchorage,*
> *In Christ his impetuous temper found restraint,*
> *In Christ his versatile personality found fulfill-*
> *ment.*"

What is your preference?

You can go the way the world points or move and go in the direction Jesus Christ gives. What is your preference?

We all can choose to use our bodies as instruments of unrighteousness and let sin reign in them OR we can choose to be found *"always bearing about in the body the dying of the Lord Jesus that the life also of Jesus may be manifest in our bodies"* (II Cor. 4:10).

May we be great for Jesus. May ours be the heroism of Savonarola to accept flame, ours be the strength of Socrates to receive the poison cup of ridicule, ours the gladness of Bunyan to enter the dungeon, ours the gratitude of Paul to endure the whips and scourge of outrageous treatment, ours the daring of Livingstone to face the lions and serpents and scorpions, ours to be crucified unto the world and the world to us, ours to bleed that we may bless, ours to lose our lives, ours to be fuel for human bonfires, ours to unyoke the tyrannies of the flesh. Ours to be hinges on great gates God shall swing, ours to take from their thrones evils coiled there like adders.

CURSE OF CONJECTURE

TEXT: *"Evil surmisings"* (I Timothy 6:4).

"Minds...destitute of the truth...supposing" (I Timothy 6:5).

With no purpose to hurt, with the desire to help, with no claim to be more Christian than others, not in despair but in distress, write I not as a know-it-all, with no desire for praise of men, and with some lamentation.

Into the vast and beautiful continent of conservative theology and Bible-loyal truth, iniquitous inroads and invasion have been made by modernistic and liberal thought, teaching and preaching. Devil-pleasing and God-displeasing assaults on the scriptural understanding of life is energetic, relentless, implicit. We have irrefutable evidence that in some schools — colleges, universities, seminaries — and some pulpits and editorial desks declarations that are invariably slanted against our orthodox spiritual heritages.

The editor of CHRISTIANITY TODAY stated this tragic fact, when he wrote: "Only a minority of philosophy departments include any competent champion of supernatural prospectives." He states that on most campuses perceptive Christian faculty members are lonely men whose Biblical convictions and teachings are assailed in university pulpits and by faculty colleagues who disparage evangelical theism as off-beat. "What one Christian professor achieves through the objective presentation of Christian views, his colleagues often destroy through distortion and ridicule."

Today, a naturalistic philosophy underlying the whole educational system of the nation provides its youth with a basis for discarding all faith in God and all sense of moral responsibility to any law except the law of their own sensuous appetites. Divorce, broken homes, and a sickening disregard for the sanctities of life appall and alarm, yet no remedy avails. Our streets are filled with men bearing the mark of Cain, and women wearing the scarlet robe of Rahab. Few hear the prophetic voice of warning — even if such a voice is raised. The whole people seem too busy going to hell happily to bother with any warners and prophetic kill-joys.

Billy Graham — godly and God-used — recently said, after visiting with young people on the nation's campuses, that he found a vacuum of religion and moral fiber developing in America.

Have not modern rationalism and liberalism, with an unawareness of the rattle of the dry bones of their conceit, attacked the deity of our Lord, His blood atonement, His virgin birth, and other vital doctrines? Have they not given undue emphasis to the doctrine of His humanity, love, perfection and example so as to produce a beautiful social Gospel — giving more importance to tradition which is the word of man in contra-distinction to the Bible, which is the word of God? Know you not that those who identify with the ecumenical movement must accept tradition as authoritative?

Is not much of our modern theology effecting hurtfully

our Southern Baptist Convention life — as we live in an age of unbelief ranging from a mind but subtle agnosticism to a blatantly arrogant atheism?

In the education which is called Christian — is not the supernatural often reduced to ignorance? In many educational areas and arenas is not the Bible summoned to appear at the bar of human reason and a "Thus saith the mind of man" substituted for a "Thus saith the Lord God"? Are not Faith's wings clipped by Reason's scissors? Are not many narratives of the Bible pilloried in unhidden doubts and ridicule?

We know, as we read some books and listen to the testimonies of some students as to what is taught in some schools that the warm wonder of Christianity is submitted to the cold and merciless analysis of Philistines of transcendent cleverness — as they label the Bible miracles myths, the reality of heaven as a place as sickly sentimentality, and belief in hell as a place the wild nightmares of disordered brains.

In our schools has our religious heritage been allowed to dwindle — since many students look upon the church as a thing of the past in a campus life that reflects world ferment? Are not many students hurtfully influenced by teachers and preachers who are exponents of logical positions or naturalism? Do not some professors who claim the Christian view misrepresent it in the anti-intellectual mood and word of Liberalism, Barthianism, existentialism, ecumenialism, neo-orthodoxy, and linguistic theology?

Do not some teachers drop jungle poison into the wells at which and from which our forefathers drank and slaked their thirst for personal righteousness? Are not there among us those who girdle the ancient trees under whose shade those who wrote history in blood before they wrote it in ink, found shelter in the "burden and heat of the day"?

The voice of neo-orthodoxy is heard among us — denying the verbal inspiration of the Bible in the sense of verbal inerrancy, accepting the critical views as to the origin of the Bible and finding legend in many parts of the synoptic Gospels, admitting many doctrinal errors in the Bible and acknowledging many doctrinal errors in the teachings of Jesus, denying the validity of any logical, historical, or experimental evidences for the existence of God? Neo-orthodoxy does not accept the authority of the Bible, nor the creation account in Genesis as fact, but prefers the theory of evolution — evolution which has caricatured, changed, cursed, and crucified the educational mind of many.

Neo-orthodoxy does not accept the New Testament teachings concerning Christ, nor the doctrine of the atonement as set forth in the New Testament nor the New Testament teachings concerning the resurrection of Christ and the return of Christ.

Are not offers made to surrender some of the most precious principles ever held by Bible Christianity? Know we not that sure-enough Baptists will never agree that the Bible is but an instrument, a witness, a channel, a record, or a sign pointing to the Word of God? We should claim that the Bible is, in all of its parts, as it claims to be — the inscripturated Word of the Living God. But do we?

Today, ECUMENICISM, "the erosion of Protestantism," a publicized minister advocates a unity which undermines the foundation of our faith — giving an advocacy of compromise on such essentials as the doctrine of God, the validity of Scriptures, the Deity of Christ, His virgin birth, His atoning and substitutionary death, His physical resurrection, and visible, literal, bodily return to the earth.

Recently, an article was published entitled "A CHURCH HISTORIAN WARNS PRESBYTERIANS ARE DEMOTING THE BIBLE." In this article, Dr. John H. Gerstner, professor of church history at Pittsburg Theological Seminary, wrote: "Never before has a church spoken of the Bible without bearing witness to its inspiration." He speaks of "heresies that lurk in the shadows of vague language." Speaking of the new Westminster Conference of Faith of 1967, he speaks of the "obfuscation of the new creed", declares that "the new creed of 1967 is saying nothing or something — if something, it is a slander of our fathers; if nothing it is an insult to us. He says: "Notwithstanding the possible soundness of the persons who composed the group who put forth the 'Confession of 1967' we appeal to them, in the name of Christ whom we all profess to love, to rescind the confession before it becomes an indelible blemish on the escutcheon of the church."

I give herewith some QUOTATIONS, which show that there are enemies of the Bible who displace fundamental facts with speculative fancies — enemies who put question marks after every great spiritual affirmation — enemies who, with supercilious pose and an air of intellectual superiority, and a skeptical attitude toward the supernatural, make maybes mighty, and plant pernicious probabilities in many young minds — sowing surmises in the field of life.

Dr. Raley once president of Oklahoma Baptist University, said: "We face a problem of paganistic order and messimistic philosophy. Out of thirty-five outstanding educators in America, who were questioned on the matter of religion, only one revealed a well defined evidence of loyalty to the Word of God"

Dr. Sanders, once president of Memphis State University said: "Our educational system seeks to make men clever without making them good. We can go from kindergarden to a Ph.D. degree and never read a line of the Bible."

Dr. Ockenga of Boston, said: "Modern mockery is centered in the intellectualism of our day. This intellectualism would confine God to natural law — refuting Bible teaching, mocking the physical resurrection and return of Christ in glory."

Note these quotations from false teaching:
George Birnie Smith: "We must, when necessary, use and modify the Bible to meet our problem."
Professor George Durant Drake: "Obviously untrue are many Bible statements."

-51-

Professor George Foster: "Man is the Book's judge — the Book is not man's judge."

Professor Morton Scot Enslin, Crozer Theological Seminary, says that the truth of the conjecture that Jesus was born of Mary fathered by a blond German soldier cannot be denied. That means Jesus was by the accident of immorality.

Ferre says: "Jesus never was nor became God."

Myron J. Hertel, who received his training at Andover Newton Baptist Theological Seminary was asked by his ordination council what he believed about the blood of Christ. His reply: "The blood of Jesus is of no more value in the salvation of a soul than the water in which Pilate washed his hands.'"

Dr. Harry Emerson Fosdick wrote: "Of course, I do not believe in the virgin birth or in the old-fashioned substitutionary doctrine of the atonement — and I do not know any intelligent person who does."

Professor Hobart. Crozier Seminary, said: "I cannot see anything understandable or acceptable in the theory that my guilt and my penalty were placed upon Christ."

Professor Vedder, once of Crozer, said: "Of all the slanders that men have perpetuated against the Most High, this doctrine of the substitutionary atonement is the most impudent and most insulting."

Dr. George Butterick, in his book "CHRISTIAN FACT AND MODERN DOUBT" says: "Probably few people who claim to believe every word of the Bible really mean it. The avowal held to its last logic would risk a trip to the insane asylum." This man, popular importation among Baptists, writes: "Jesus apparently conquered death, but we do not know. Why pretend we do?"

Concerning such men and such statements, I quote Dr. B. H. Carroll, who, speaking of those who try to account for everything in the Bible without recourse to the supernatural, said: "No man who denies the supernatural has the right to try to expound the Bible." He also said: "The prevalent evils of today arise from the fact that children of Belial occupy many pulpits and many chairs in the theological seminaries and Christian schools. Always they are the advance couriers of disaster to God's cause."

Note some things which have been taught in some schools under the guise of scholarship: "The fish did not swallow Jonah." "Noah did not have an ark." "The flood was probably a disastrous flood in Babylon.""Methusaleh's long life was incompatible with the physical structure." "Melchisedeck was not a priest of God." "Moses on Mt. Sinai was only a dramatic picture founded on a thunder storm." "Adam dreamed about the rib being taken from his side to make a helpmeet for him." "The tree of knowledge of good and evil was some sort of vegetable poison — a sort of poison ivy." "The story of the fall is a parable based on ancient literary symbolism." "Manna — a white secretion from the Tamarisk tree." "Death of Ussah — either the cart turned over on him and crushed him or he was stricken with a heart attack." "Adam and Eve were driven out of the garden by a terrible thunderstorm." "Bible writers had unbalanced minds and rabid imaginations." "Daniel never was in a lion's den." "Mary mistook the angel Gabriel for a passing stranger." "Jesus did not walk on the water, but walked on the shore and the disciple thought He was walking on the water." "Jesus fainted on the cross and when He was taken down, He was not dead but in a swoon. The coolness of the tomb revived Him — and He escaped, appeared to his disciples, but died soon afterward."

Listen to some blatant and blasphemous voices on the Highway of Modernism:

Dr. Thomas Altizer, Emory University, said: "God is dead. He died when Jesus died on the cross. He is not simply hidden from view. He is dead!"

Prof. Harvey Cox of Harvard's Divinity School has said:

> "We must learn to speak of God in a secular
> fashion. It will do us no good to cling to our

religious and metaphysical versions of Christianity in the hope that one day religion will once again be back. Religion is disappearing forever, and that means we can now let go and emerse ourselves in the new world, of the secular city. The starting point for any theology of today must be a theology of social change."

Dr. E.E. Aubrey, president of Crozer Seminary, has said: "Modern conceptions of God all tend to make Him something other than a superman....."
Dr. C.W. Reese has said: "As far as I am concerned, the idea of God plays no important part in my religion."

A liberal who once taught in one of our Christian schools, said: "Where the old religion made the supreme object God, the new religion makes it humanity; sociology is now taking the place of theology and the world hope of an improved social order is replacing the belief in life after death."

A Washington scientist has said: "God, if anything, is hydrogen and carbon."

A funeral service for God was conducted at a Methodist College in North Carolina. The chorus sang: "Your God is Dead! He died because you held his hand too tightly."

In the obituary column of an Atlanta newspaper the death of God was officially announced. The column read: "God, creator of the universe, ultimate reality of Christians, died late yesterday morning during major surgery undertaken to correct a massive diminishing influence."

Modernism says: "The Bible is a myth." "Prophecy at its best is human guess work."

Prof. Pratt has said, "The Bible has lost all hold on the leaders of thought and is destined before many years to become one of the curiosities of the past. The inspiration of those who spake a "Thus saith the Lord' is only a little higher type than that of the heathen medicine man."

The Reverend Malcolm Boyd of the Episcopal church

performed all of his sermons in a nightclub style. He wrote a book of prayers entitled: "Are you Running With Me Jesus?". Reverend Boyd said: "I am trying to knock off some of the academic dry rot."

Prof. G.B. Smith: "May we not demand that God shall be required to receive the moral reproval of men? The spirit of democracy protests against such ideas that God has a right to insist on some rigid plan of salvation."

Prof. Coe of Union Theological Seminary, has said: "Religion is holy within the natural psychological order. The joy which often accompanies conversion is nothing more or less than the effect of religious laughing gas."

Dr. C.B. Lockwood has said: "Every honest man knows that there is no supernatural regeneration, conversion, or salvation."

The philosophy of *Horace Bushnell* is being accepted without question. He says: "To become a Christian is a mere matter of learning and has nothing at all to do with conversion."

Prof. Soares has said: "Redemption is an absolute fancy. We refuse the idea that the principle business of the church is to get people converted."

These Bible critics who summon the Bible to appear at the bar of human reason, remind me of a rill sitting in judgment on the volume of a river, of a candle summoning the sun to appear for judgment for not being bright enough, or a stagnant pond summoning an ocean to judgment for being too shallow.

All of which brings us to ask if teachers in our seminaries and colleges are holding the line for a Biblical conservative rather than a liberal theology? Does any teaching and preaching today burglarize with evil vandalism the house of Faith? Do not many of the moral disorders we find in modern life — broken promises, broken homes, quick divorces, juvenile delinquency, crimes of violence against the person, booze debaucheries, Ingersolic unbelief — come to birth and grow to a life of rampage because of a watered down perverted theology and Christless education? With anguish of heart, I ask this question.

In this day when so many things make the Bible-loving heart sick, there are tears and travail, disaster and disease, defeat and despair, gropers in darkness, grovelers in the grossness of animal appetites, degraders of the body, and Ichabod writers on the doors of some houses and temples of worship and capitals of governments.

Is our moral mess in any way the result of the iniquitous inroads of modern theology in the spiritual life of this nation? How deeply is it affecting our own Baptist life? We are living in an age of unbelief, ranging from a mild but subtle agnosticism to a blatant atheism, from which many suffer to some extent from this thing which is daily in the air we breathe. How far does this unbelief which is so general in all the realms of our life — home, church, school, business, nation — hinder our efforts in evangelism and cause in part our decline in baptisms?

Dr. Vance Havner — always wise and Christian — says: "Today, in a day of doctrinal fogs and moral twilights, we have summit conferences with the Canaanites instead of standing on Carmel with Elijah. No wonder we see no revival rain in this famished land. The showdown must come before the showers."

Evils are inevitable when teachers calmly mutilate our only reliable franchise of Christian hope — stating that the Bible is filled with inaccuracies, substituting human speculations for the revealed pronouncements of God.

What but evil can come from the preaching and teaching which brings about religion without the Holy Ghost, forgiveness without repentance, politics without God, Christianity without Christ, Heaven without hell, the Bible without divine inspiration?

Jeremiah described many today when he said: "The wise men have rejected the Word of the Lord — and what wisdom is in them?" (Jeremiah 8:9).

I fear that there are those — teachers, preachers,

writers, — among Southern Baptists who, careless as to the consequences of their uncertainty about Bible certainties, mount their steeds named Probably and Perhaps, and, with the frenzy of "lit-up" cowboys who "shoot up the town," or, with the cool deliberation of bushwhackers, ride with irreverence over the main articles of the Christian faith proclaimed by Whitfield, Wesley, Spurgeon, Broughton, Dodd, Broadus, Sampey, Carroll, Scarborough, Talmage, Truett, and others no less faithful to the Bible.

I fear we have among us in pulpit and teacher-chair positions those who refrain from making direct and brazen denial so much and so often, but do not hesitate to put a question mark after many Bible affirmations — calling many claims of Christianity church yard ghosts.

Dr. Truett once asked: "Do you not agree that much of our current preaching is too newspaperish? That it is too much given to little scraps of discussion about the transient and superficial? That it does not stretch out into the eternities? That it fails to have the tone of the preaching of God's Book? We are not primarily to be social agitators or reformers."

What the Apostle Peter wrote by the Holy Ghost is true today: *"But there were false prophets also among the people, even as there shall be false teachers among you, who privily shall bring upon themselves swift destruction"* (II Peter 2:1).

Such forget, if they ever knew, that you can no more demonstrate Christian truth with a syllogism than you can draw music out of an organ with a corkscrew — no more than you can gather sunbeams with a carpet sweeper.

Believing that the Southern Baptist Convention is the greatest evangelical body on this earth, concerned with the welfare of all our churches and institutions and missionary endeavours in many lands, I say we, even all of us, should stand for doctrinal truths and Bible affirmations with the Orange — in the thirty-seven-year war. King Phillip of Spain offered him fabulous sums to surrender — offered to place him in line for the Spanish throne. But Prince William sent back the message which has been embalmed in the hearts of Dutch people and inscribed imperishable upon the pages of history; "Not for wife, nor children, nor lands, nor life will I mix in my cup one drop of treason."

I would that in all our schools, from high school to seminary, without exception, all teachers would say that not for endowment, nor expansion, nor new dormitories, nor academic lustre, nor fame, nor money, will we mix in our huge cup one drop of sceptism, or infidelic liberalism or any denials or disparagements or ridicule of Bibical assertion and affirmations.

THE THREES
OF THE TREES

TEXT:
"Christ...who did no sin...who, when he was reviled, reviled not again; when he suffered, he threatened not; but committed himself to him that judgeth righteously: who his own self bare our sins in his own body on the tree, that we, being dead to sins, should live unto righteousness: by whose stripes ye were healed" (I Peter 2:23-24).

_5_

In life there are three periods — birth, life, death — the cradle, the course, the coffin. Yes — childhood, youth, old age. The human body is made up of flesh, bones, blood.

In time, there are three times — past, present, future. In a day — there are three parts, morning, noon , night. In motion — three speeds: moderate, slow, fast. In a book — three parts: introduction, contents, conclusion. In measurements, three dimensions: length, breadth, thickness. In water, three states — liquid, ice, steam. In grammar — three genders: masculine, feminine, neuter. As to the world's zones, there are three — torrid, temperate, frigid. As to God, there are three persons — God the Father, Christ, the Son; The Holy Spirit.

In life we find that THREES figure largely. We have Newton's three laws of motion. In the Greek language, we have three members: singular, dual, plural. In mathematics, there are three chief signs — plus, minus, equality. In language, there are three persons — first, second, third. In music, there are three things to distinguish tones — loudness, pitch, quality. In our lives, there are three realities necessary to life — eating, drinking, breathing. In every civilization, there are three periods — potamic, thessalic, oceanic.

And the number THREE has significance in the Bible. The number THREE in the Bible stands for everything that is solid, real, substantial, complete and entire.

THREE in the natural world and the world of things material is the complete and entire number. All things especially complete are stamped with this number.

THREE is the first geometrical number. Two straight lines cannot possibly enclose any space or form a solid.

THREE lines are necessary as the dimensions of length, breadth, and heighth are required to form a solid.

THREE is the symbol of the cube — the simplest form of a solid figure.

There are three great dimensions of time — and by the three time is complete and completed. These times are past, present, future.

Three degrees of comparison express the sum total of our knowledge of qualities — good, better, best. Three kingdoms include and complete all man's knowledge of matter — mineral, vegetable, animal.

Three functions express and complete the sum of human capability — and these three are thought, word and deed.

God's attributes are three. Complete in Him and with Him only are there three — omniscience, omnipresence, and omnipotence.

In the Scriptures, the number THREE denotes Divine perfection and completeness. It indicates what is real, substantial, complete, and Divine. It is the number of Divine fulness and the number of resurrection.

The number THREE occurs in the Bible for the first time at Genesis 1:13: *"And the evening and the morning was the third day"*. On this third day was the day when not only was the earth caused to rise up out of the water as a symbol and type of life in Christ, but also life was seen coming up out of the place of the dead. *"And God said, Let the earth bring forth grass, the herb yielding seed, and the fruit tree yielding fruit after his kind, whose seed is in itself, upon the earth: and it was so"* (Genesis 1:11).

It was the "life from the dead" day or resurrection day. Jesus rose from the dead on the third day. This is carefully maintained and sustained throughout the Scriptures.

> *"But he answered and said unto them an evil and adulterous generation seeketh after a sign; and there shall no sign be given to it, but the sign of the prophet Jonas: For as Jonas was three days and three nights in the whale's belly; so shall the Son of man be three days and three nights in the heart of the earth"* (Matt. 12:39-40).

> *"And when the people were gathered thick together, he began to say, This is an evil generation: they seek a sign; and there shall no sign be given it, but the sign of Jonas the prophet"* (Luke 11:29).

> *"Now the Lord had prepared a great fish to swallow up Jonah. And Jonah was in the belly of the fish three days and three nights"* (Jonah 1:17).

Jesus Himself raised three people from the dead. They were the twelve-year-old daughter of Jairus, a ruler of the synagogue (Luke 8:41-42, 49-55). And the son of the widow of Nain (Luke 7:12-15). And Lazarus, brother of Martha and Mary of Bethany town (John 11:41-44).

On the third day, Jesus was "perfected". This is the meaning of three. *"And he said unto them, Go ye, and tell that fox, Behold I cast out devils, and I do cures today and tomorrow, and the third day I shall be perfected"* (Luke 13:32).

Jesus was crucified the third hour of the day. For THREE hours — the sixth to the ninth — He was enclosed in darkness like a shroud.

> *"And it was about the sixth hour, and there was darkness over all the earth until the ninth hour. And the sun was darkened, and the veil of the temple was rent in the midst"* (Luke 23:44-45).

The inscriptions on His cross were of THREE languages — showing the completeness of man's rejection of Jesus Christ.

> *"And Pilate wrote a title and put it on the cross. And the writing was JESUS OF NAZARETH THE KING OF THE JEWS. This title then read many of the Jews: for the place where Jesus was crucified was nigh to the city: and it was written in Hebrew, and Greek, and Latin"* (John 19:19-20).

Let us recall here that there are THREE persons in the Godhead — Father, Son and Holy Ghost.

THREE times the Seraphims cry, "Holy, Holy, Holy" as the prophet Isaiah sits in the Temple. They cry "Holy" one time each for the THREE persons. The priestly blessing upon the children of Israel was threefold with doubtless, a reference to Father, Son, and Holy Ghost. The Lord "bless", the Lord "make", the Lord "lift".

> *"The Lord bless thee, and keep thee:*
> *The Lord make his face shine upon thee, and be gracious unto thee:*
> *The Lord lift up His countenance upon thee, and give thee peace"* (Numbers 6:24-26).

There were THREE great feasts in the calendar of Israel: Unleavened Bread, Weeks, Tabernacle. *"Three times in a year shall all thy males appear before the Lord they God in the place which he shall choose; in the feast of unleavened bread, and the feast of weeks, and in the feast of tabernacles: and they shall not appear before the Lord empty:"* (Deut. 16:16).

Jesus sums up the writings of the Old Testament under THREE divisions — the Law, the Prophets, the Psalms.

> *"And he said unto them, These are the words which I spake unto you, while I was yet with you, that all things must be fulfilled, which were written in the law of Moses, and in the prophets, and in the psalms, concerning me"* (Luke 24:44).

The river Jordan, the "river of miracles" was THREE times miraculously divided.

Joshua 4:7 tells us: *"The waters of Jordan were cut off before the Ark of the Covenant."*

> *"And Elijah took his mantle, and wrapped it together, and smote the waters and they were divided hither and thither, so that they two went over on dry ground. And he took the mantle of Elijah that fell from him, and smote the waters, and said Where is the Lord God of Elijah? And when he also had smitten the waters, they parted hither and thither: and Elijah went over"* (II Kings 2:8 and 14). *Elisha*

There was instituted a three-day search for Elijah and this was conclusive evidence that he could not be found: *"And when they urged him till he was ashamed, he said, Send. They sent therefore fifty men; and they sought three days, Kings 2:17).*

In the book of Jude the completeness of apostasy is stated by a reference to three examples —*"the way of Cain", "the error of Balaam," "the gainsaying of Korah"* (Jude 1:11).

Moreover, there are three gifts of Grace — Faith, Hope, Love.

Temptation is expressed through a three-fold nature — the lust of the flesh, the lust of the eyes, the pride of life.

THREE things our first parents saw at the tree — *"Good for food," "pleasant to the eyes," "desired to make one wise "* (Genesis 3:6).

Man has THREE great enemies — the World, the Flesh, the Devil.

Three things are predicted of God in John's Epistle *"God is LOVE," "God is SPIRIT," "God is LIGHT."*

Three times God gave the commandment *"Ask of me"* — *to* Solomon (I Kings 3:5), Ahaz (Isaiah 7:11), to Messiah (Psalms 2:8).

THREE times God's testimony unto Christ came in a voice from heaven and we read: *"And lo a voice from heaven, saying, This is my beloved Son, in whom I am well pleased"* (Matt. 3:17). *"While he yet spake, behold, a bright cloud overshadowed them: and behold a voice out of the cloud, which said, This is my beloved Son, in whom I am well pleased; hear ye him"* (Matt. 17:5). *"Father, glorify thy name. Then came there a voice from heaven, saying, I have both glorified it, and will glorify it again"* (John 12:28. Israel was completely separated from Egypt by a THREE-day journey into the wilderness. Pharaoh desired much less distance.

"And Pharaoh called for Moses and for Aaron, and said, Go ye, sacrifice to your God in the land" (Exodus 8:25).

The official glory of Christ is THREEfold — Prophet, Priest, King.

When God would in fullness of testimony concerning the admission of Gentiles into the Church, He let the sheet down THREE times to Peter.

"This was done thrice: and the vessel was received up again into heaven" (Acts 10:16).

-66-

Consider this list of names as they appear in triplet — and with what completeness and co-ordination they present.

Shem, Ham, Japheth.

Abraham, Isaac, Jacob.

Gershon, Kohath, and Meran.

Saul, David, Solomon.

Noah, Daniel, Job.

Shadrach, Meshach, Abednego.

Pilate, James, John.

Those, with many other instances of the use of the number THREE are an evidence of its numerical and spiritual significance. The occurrence of number THREE is not fanciful, not forced, not foolish. It speaks of the accuracy of the Word of God and of its perfection. "Thy Word is perfect."

But we, after quite a lengthy introduction, must think of "THE TREE" — as the Apostle Peter calls the cross. And that tree is the place where the history of human guilt culminates; where the purposes of divine love are made intelligible; where the majesty of the law is vindicated; where the fires of hell are extinguished for the believer; where Satan's head is bruised; where the fountain of salvation is revoked; where the hangman's noose is taken from our wrists; where the devil's yoke is taken from necks.

We come to consider

I - CHRIST PUT TO DEATH

The death of Jesus Christ, the Son of God, is the central event of our world's history. It is the only cure for the curse — the curse of evil that dooms human beings to misery.

We can all say what the Apostle Paul said: *"Christ loved me and gave Himself for me"* (Galatians 2:20).

Christ was put to death (1) BY wicked men.

"Which of the prophets have not your fathers persecuted? And they have slain them which shewed before of the coming of the Just One; of

whom ye have been now the betrayers and murderers" (Acts 7:52).

Christ was put to death (2) FOR wicked men.

"For when we were yet without strength, in due time Christ died for the ungodly. For scarcely for a righteous man will one die: yet peradventure for a good man some would even dare to die. But God commendeth his love toward us, in that, while we were yet sinners, Christ died for us" (Romans 5:6-8).

We see the kind of folks for whom Jesus died — when we see what sin is like. Sin is compared to the uncleanness of the dog. "As a dog returneth to his vomit, so a fool returneth to his folly" (Proverbs 26:11).

Sin is compared to serpents and poisonous vipers. "Ye serpents, ye generation of vipers, how can ye escape the damnation of hell?" (Matt. 23:33).

Sin is compared to the fierceness of the leopard. "After this I beheld, and lo another, like a leopard, which had upon the back of it four wings of a fowl; the beast had also four heads and dominion was given it" (Daniel 7:6).

Sin is compared to a ravenous lion. "They gaped upon me with their mouths as a ravening and a roaring lion" (Psalms 22:13).

Sin is compared to the cunning of the fox. "Go ye and tell that fox, Behold, I cast out devils, and I do cures today and tomorrow, and the third day I shall be perfected" (Luke 13:32).

Sin is compared to the wallowing of the sow. "But it is happened unto them according to the true proverb, The dog is turned to his own vomit again; and the sow that was washed to her wallowing in the mire" (II Peter 2:22).

Sin is compared to the mercilessness of the boar. "The boar out of the wood doth waste it, and the wild beast of the field doth devour it" (Psalms 80:13).

Sin is compared to the devouring of the wolf. "But he

that is an hireling, and not the shepherd, whose own tne sheep are not, seeth the wolf coming, and leaveth the sheep and fleeth; and the wolf catcheth them, and scattereth the sheep" (John 10:12).

Sin is compared to the stupidity of the sheep. *"All we like sheep have gone astray; we have turned every one to his own way; and the Lord hath laid on him the iniquity of us all"* (Isa. 53:6).

Sin is compared to the stubbornness of a donkey. *"For vain man would be wise, though man be born like a wild ass's colt"* (Prov. 11:12).

We note now that Jesus died (3) WITH wicked men.

"And when they were come to the place, which is called Calvary, there they crucified him, and the malefactors, one on the right hand and the other on the left" (Luke 23:33).

"But the other answering rebuked him, saying, dost not thou fear God, seeing thou art in the same condemnation? And we indeed justly; for we receive the due reward of our deeds; but this man hath done nothing amiss" (Luke 23:40-41).

In thinking of Christ's death, we think of

II - CHRIST CRUCIFIED

Christ was crucified for ALL. *"Who gave himself a ransom for all, to be testified in due time"* (I Timothy 2:6).

Christ was crucified for US. *"Who gave himself for us, that he might redeem us from all iniquity, and purify unto himself a peculiar people, zealous of good works"* (Titus 2:14).

Christ was crucified for ME. *"I am crucified with Christ: nevertheless I live yet not I, but Christ liveth in me; and the life which I now live in the flesh, I live by the faith of the Son of God, who loved me, and gave himself for me"* (Gal. 2:20).

As to Christ's crucifixion we give thought to

III - THREE "IFS"

There is the "if" of the rulers. *"And the people stood beholding. And the rulers also with them derided him, saying, He saved others; let him save himself, if he be Christ, the chosen of God"* (Luke 23:35).

There is the "if" of the soldiers. *"And the soldiers also mocked him, coming to him, and offering him vinegar, and saying, If thou be the king of the Jews, save thyself"* (Luke 23:36-37).

There is the "if" of the criminals. *"And one of the malefactors which were hanged railed on him, saying, If thou be Christ, save thyself and us"* (Luke 23:39).

In thinking of Christ's death, we must think of the

IV - THREE CROSSES OR THREE TREES.

On one cross was the penitent thief — sin IN him, not ON him. *"But the other answering rebuked him, saying, Dost not thou fear God, seeing thou art in the same condemnation?"* (Luke 23:40). *"And Jesus said unto him, Verily I say unto thee, Today shalt thou be with me in paradise"* (Luke 23:43).

On one cross was the impenitent thief — sin IN him and ON him. *"And one of the malefactors which were hanged railed on him, saying, If thou be Christ, save thyself and us"* (Luke 23:39).

This makes us think of this truth:

> *"And the fifth angel poured out his vial upon the seat of the beast: and his kingdom was full of darkness; and they gnawed their tongues for pain, and blasphemed the God of heaven because of their pains and their sores, and repented not of their deeds"* (Revelation 16:10-11).

On one cross was Jesus Hominum Salvator — sin ON Him, not IN Him. *"And a superscription also was written over him in letters of Greek, and Latin, and Hebrew, THIS*

IS THE KING OF THE JEWS" (Luke 23:38). *"For he hath made him to be sin for us, who knew no sin; that we might be made the righteousness of God in him"* (II Cor. 5:21).

Yes, there were THREE trees on Calvary.

On one tree one died FOR sin; that was Jesus.

On one tree one died IN sin; that was the impenitent thief.

On one tree one died saved FROM sin; that was the penitent thief.

One died in SACRIFICE; that was Jesus.

One died in SCORN; that was the impenitent thief.

One died in SALVATION; that was the penitent thief.

One died a BENEFACTOR; that was Jesus.

One died a BLASPHEMER; that was the impenitent thief.

One died a BELIEVER; that was the penitent thief.

One tree was the tree of REDEMPTION — the tree on which Jesus died.

One tree was the tree of REJECTION — the tree on which the impenitent man died.

One tree was the tree of RECEPTION — the tree on which the penitent thief died.

One tree yielded holy and saving BLOOD — the tree on which Jesus died.

One tree yielded awful BRIARS — of refusal — the tree on which the impenitent man died.

One tree yielded BLOSSOMS — more beautiful than Aaron's rod that blossomed. *"And it came to pass, that on the morrow Moses went into the tabernacle of witness; and, behold, the rod of Aaron for the house of Levi was budded, and brought forth buds, and bloomed blossoms, and yielded almonds"* (Numbers 17:8). That tree blossomed with the blossoms of faith.

At Christ's death were

V - THREE SUPERNATURAL SIGNS

(1) There was BLOOD.

"But one of the soldiers with a spear pierced his side, and forthwith came there out blood and water" (John 19:34).

(2) There was darkness and the rent veil.

"And it was about the sixth hour, and there was a darkness over all the earth until the ninth hour. And the sun was darkened, and the veil of the temple was rent in the midst" (Luke 23:44-45).

"Having therefore, brethren, boldness to enter into the holiest by the blood of Jesus, by a new and living way, which he hath consecrated for us, through the veil, that is to say, his flesh;" (Hebrews 10:19-20).

(3) There was the RENDING of the ROCKS. Creation moved.

"And, behold, the veil of the temple was rent in twain from the top to the bottom and the earth did quake, and the rocks rent;" (Matt. 27:51).

"God also bearing them witness, both with signs and wonders, and with divers miracles, and gifts of the Holy Ghost, according to his own will?" (Hebrews 2:4).

"And to Jesus the mediator of the new covenant, and to the blood of sprinkling, that speaketh better things than that of Abel. See that ye refuse not him that speaketh for if they escaped not who refused him that spake on earth, much more shall not we escape, if we turn away from him that speaketh from heaven:" (Heb. 12:24-25).

And GRAVES were opened — manifesting the first fruits of the resurrection power. *"After His resurrection...appeared unto many:"*

"And the graves were opened; and many bodies of the saints arose..." (Matt. 27:52).

Note now the

VI - THREE WORDS OF THE PENITENT DYING THIEF

In his words there was SELF-CONDEMNATION. "We indeed are suffering justly." In other words, we merit what we are receiving. The thorns we pluck are of our own planting. The fire that burns we kindled. *"And we indeed justly; for we receive the due reward of our deeds:"* (Luke 23:41).

In his words there was JUSTIFICATION for Jesus. *"But this man has done nothing amiss"* (Luke 23:41). That is what all the world must say. Men putting Him under their microscopes of scrutiny. Men putting Him under their spectographs of investigation. Men putting Him under their telescopes of observation — ALL have to say: "He has done nothing amiss." ALL must say that he never struck a jarring note, never made a misstep, never hurried before popularity, never halted before antagonism, never was betrayed into an error of judgment, never was anything but holiness incarnate.

In his words there was the ACKNOWLEDGEMENT OF Christ as Lord.

"And he said unto Jesus, Lord, remember me when thou comest into thy kingdom" (Luke 23:42).

Many are willing to call Jesus a great teacher, a great philosopher, a great benefactor, a good man. But they are not willing to call him Lord.

"That at the name of Jesus every knee should bow, of things in heaven and things in earth, and things under the earth; and that every tongue should confess that Jesus Christ is Lord, to the glory of God the Father" (Phil. 2:10-11).

But Jesus said:

> "For the Father judgeth no man, but hath committed all judgment unto the Son: That all men should honour the Son, even as they honour the Father. He that honoureth not the Son honoureth not the Father which hath sent him" (John 5:22-23).

You lay the corner stone of a building in which Jesus is ignored, you honor not God. You have a meeting of Protestants, Baptists, Catholics, Jews in which the name of Jesus is omitted in the prayers — and God is not honored.

VII - CHRIST'S ANSWER

1. *"Today"* (Luke 23:43).

Not "tomorrow" but "today". Not "some other time" but "NOW". *"While it is said, Today if ye will hear his voice, harden not your hearts, as in the provocation"* (Hebrews 3:15).

2. *"Shalt thou be with me"* (Luke 23:43).

"With me". With perfect love, with perfect wisdom, with perfect mercy, utter holiness.

> "For I am in a strait betwixt two, having a desire to depart, and to be with Christ; which is far better" (Phil. 1:23).

3. *"In Paradise"* (Luke 23:43).

> "He that hath an ear, let him hear what the Spirit saith unto the churches; To him that overcometh will I give to eat of the tree of life, which is in the midst of the paradise of God" (Revelation 2:7).

We should not forget the

VIII - THREE-PART INSCRIPTION

> "And Pilate wrote a title, and put it on the cross. And the writing was, JESUS OF NAZARETH

THE KING OF THE JEWS. This title then read many of the Jews: for the place where Jesus was crucified was nigh to the city; and it was written in Hebrew, and Greek, and Latin" (John 19:19-20).

This was a tri-lingual inscription. The Hebrew language stood for religion, Greek language for literature and arts, Latin-Roman language for law and government. The word "JESUS" means Saviour in any language. "Whosoever will!"

"And the Spirit and the bride say, Come. And let him that heareth say, Come. And let him that is athirst come. And whosoever will, let him take the water of life freely" (Revelation 22:17).

Always there is one single fact that we may oppose to all rhetoric , arguments and adverse attitudes, scoffers and sneerers of infidelity — namely, that no man was ever sorry for OR ever repented of being a Christian on his death-bed. No man ever repented of going to the cross when he lay on his death-bed.

In His body, Jesus died for us — through the eternal Spirit offering Himself without spot to God.

In like manner, we, too, can not perform God's service to men, apart from our bodies. We need them to serve others. We need them to perform the will of God. To do this, we must give our bodies over to the Lord. Then the body becomes the instrument of God's will. It means a daily dying of self — saying NO to the lusts of the flesh — all our members absolutely and solely at the disposal of God.

When — years ago — the old speaker of the House of Parliment was arrested, his arrestors demanded of him to tell where the members of the House of Parliment were. The old man, speaker of the House of Parliment, said: "I have no eyes to see, no ears to hear, no mouth to speak, no hands to work, no feet to walk save as directed by Parliment."

May such be our courageous devotion to Jesus in the midst of this crooked and perverse and adulterous generation.

THROUGH A THIEF'S EYES

"Lord, remember me when thou comest into thy Kingdom" — (Luke 23:42) — the dying thief.

"Save thyself, and come down from the cross" — (Mark 15:30) — the mob.

6

Would I have you see Jesus through the eyes of the Sanhedrin? No — for the Sanhedrin, through envious eyes, saw him as a deceiver.

Through the eyes of the Roman soldiers? No — for they, through military eyes, utterly blind indeed, saw him as a victim.

Through the eyes of Annas? No — for Annas, through degenerate eyes, saw him as a disturbing and despised Galilean.

Through the eyes of Caiaphas? No — for Caiaphas, through ambitious eyes, saw him as a blasphemer.

Through Pilate's eyes? No — for Pilate through amazed and perplexed and irresolute eyes, saw him only as an innocent man.

Through Herod's eyes? No — for Herod, through lustful and superficial eyes, saw him as a miracle worker only, as a worker of magic.

Through the eyes of the materialistic Sadducees? No — for they, through ceremonial eyes, saw him a disseminator of repugnant resurrection doctrines.

Through the eyes of the women who lamented him? No — for they, through eyes swollen with weeping, saw him as just a poor prisoner.

Through the eyes of the disciples? No — for the disciples, even they, that dark day, believed his kingdom had shrunk to the narrow dimensions of a grave.

Through the eyes of them that stood far off smiting upon their breasts? No — for they, through awestruck eyes, saw him as an offender against Rome.

Through his mother's eyes? No — not even through her tearwashed, pain smitten eyes.

Through the eyes of Joseph of Arimathea? No — not through his timid eyes.

Through the eyes of Nicodemus? No — not through his investigative eyes.

Then — through whose eyes? Through the eyes of the malefactor who, in the throes of death, saw that in Christ's salvation there are no priestly secrets. Through the thief's eyes would I have men see Jesus today. And I am not guilty of a mad freak of stubborn ignorance — not the victim of the wild nightmare of a disordered brain in so saying.
Yes, through the eyes of him who had wasted the precious opportunities of living — through the eyes of him who had, by evil doing, set upon his own brow the crown of infamy — through the eyes of him who was a common felon, a mere ruin of a man concious of the stigma that was upon him. Thus shall we see realities more wondrous than when, looking through the microscopic lens, we see a world in a drop of water — realities more marvelous than when, using the telescope, we view landscapes fifteen million miles away

— realities more wondrous than when, looking into a spectograph, we learn the constituent elements of the remotest astral bodies, the gold in the sun, the copper in Mars, the iron on the moons of Jupiter. For to him, this dying thief, was it given to enter the unseen world hand in hand with him who holds the keys of Death and hell.

And why? Why through the thief's eyes? Because, as our two-sentence text teaches, in that hour when friend and acquaintance are put far away from the dying Redeemer, in that hour when even the familiar friend had lifted up his hand against him, in that hour when the world is one bitter voice shrieking with all the fury of hell and all the hatred of earth against him, he saw Jesus as the head-wagging, hooting mob did not see him when it howled, "Save thyself, and come down from the cross."

I - THE MOB SAW JESUS AS THE AUTHOR OF A FALSE RELIGION AND THE THIEF SAW JESUS AS THE EXEMPLAR OF THE TRUE RELIGION

The mob, calling him fool and visionary, saw Jesus as the author of a false, condemnatory religion.

Did Jesus condemn their cautious creeds, lacking devotional vitality?

Did he scorch with burning words their self-righteousness?

Did he hurl verbal thunderbolts at their street-corner prayers made for pretense?

Did he apply the torch to their ritualistic shows utterly void of inward reality?

Did he use the sword against their superficial mental illumination that lacked the urge of sacrificial passion?

Did he call them hypocrites who shut the kingdom of Heaven against men?

Did he blast with lightning-fierce words their hell-pleasing proselyting — their gnat-straining, camel-swallowing, blind guidance?

Did he uncover their inward rottenness that dwelt and

smelt like carrion beneath beauty? He did!

And because Jesus tore their masks away, they said he was a deceiver, a glutton, a winebibber, a devil. They said his false religion was too all-inclusive, defiling itself by unchaste association, by numbering outcast women among its exponents. He ate with publicans. He was the guest of sinners. He raked the gutter for his saints. He was just a carpenter's son preposterously claiming to be the Son of God. He chose illiterate fishermen and despised tax-gatherers to preach the follies of his false religion. All this — and more — they said.

But the thief, seeing not as the mob saw, saw Jesus as the exemplar of the only religion that offers redemption and salvation to all men.

He saw that the silence of Jesus was superior to the mockery of the rulers, that Christ's majestic calm gave hint of an unearthly greatness. This thief, the air hideous all around with invective, endorsed the verdict upon himself, but declared Jesus innocent.

He saw Jesus as the Good Shepherd giving his life for the lost sheep.

He saw Jesus as the Great Physician mighty to heal the diseases of the soul.

He saw Jesus as the Friend of the outcast.

He saw Jesus as the Lamb of God giving his life as a ransom for many!

He saw Jesus as One who, in life, in death, proved that God's unfathomed love is greater than man's sin and folly — in life, in death — proved that there is a wideness in God's mercy like the wideness of the sea. Yea, though the thief saw late, yet at last he saw. And, as he spoke in praise amid the mockings and jeers of the mob, his was the one voice which attested him Redeemer when all had forsaken him and fled. His was the tortured voice which was the one note of sweetness in the wild, unmusical discord. His was the voice, though the voice of a malefactor, for whose evil deeds there is neither apology nor defense, which was the one cry of faith in the hour of infinite denial and rejection.

Would that those who know not Christ, save as the historical Christ, would see him as that thief saw him that dread day on Calvary. Would that those behind whom beautiful dreams lie moulding in the muck, could see him through the eyes of the thief. Would that those before whom yawn pits of black despair, could see Jesus through the eyes of the thief. Know ye not, O souls, that Jesus makes flowers and fruits to come amid the ashes of a misspent life? Know ye not that he restores the years the locusts have eaten? Know ye not that Jesus accepts the surrendered desert and makes it blossom as the rose? Know ye not that Christ makes a man a new creature, hating things he once loved, loving things he once hated? Know ye not that he taketh man's feet out of the horrible pit, out of the miry clay, placing them on the solid rock, putting a new song in man's mouth, establishing his goings? Know ye not that while an act of crime may defile a human soul, it can leave no stain which Christ cannot remove? Know ye not that he can so change the thief as to enable him, after years of nights of burglary, to sleep the guileless sleep of toil beneath an honest roof? Know ye not that he can so lift up the harlot as to cause her to possess and maintain the purity which was hers when, with innocent eyes, she prayed at her mother's knee? Look thou through the eyes of the dying malefactor and know this blessed truth!

II - THE MOB SAW JESUS AS A HELPLESS ONE AND THE THIEF SAW JESUS AS THE HELPER OF THE HELPLESS.

The railing mob thought he was helpless, held by the nails, impotent to remove them. "And they that passed by reviled him, wagging their heads, and saying, Thou that destroyest the temple, and buildest it in three days, save thyself!" Bitter invective, ribald laughter — hissed with the venom of the adder, shouted with the levity of a clown, guffawed with the harshness and contempt of blasphemy.

"If thou be the Son of God, come down from the cross!"

Too helpless to help himself — to evade their venom. Thus they saw Jesus. *"Likewise also the chief priests mocking him, with the scribes and the elders, said, He saved others; himself he cannot save. If he be the King of Israel, let him come down from the cross, and we will believe him. He trusted in God, let him deliver him now, if he will have him; for he said, I am the Son of God"* (Mark 15:31-32).

They knew he was suffering, but they thought he was unable to lift his crown of thorns from the vein-punctured brow. They knew the nails that held him to the wood caused awful pain; but they believed he had no power to release himself. Watching his quivering body, they saw him as a victim powerless to prevent a pang of pain. Helpless he, in their sight, as a bird in the fowler's net. Helpless he, through their eyes, as a butterfly in a spider's web, as a doe in the coils of a boa-constrictor. Helpless he, by the judgment of their hard eyes, as a lamb amid wolves, as a sparrow in an eagle's talons. He could build the Temple in three days, but he could not come down from the cross! As they looked upon him whom they had pierced, they saw not that sin laid the cross on him — knew not that love held him on the cross.

But the thief saw Jesus as the Helper of the helpless, as a very present help in the time of trouble, as one who comforts when all comforts fail and helps when all helpers flee — as one who, for the helpless, brings low mountains, exalts valleys, makes crooked places straight, rough places plain, the rocks to give water and the skies bread in the desert. In this attitude the thief said: "Other refuge have I none; hangs my helpless soul on Thee."

This dying thief, looked upon by the crucifiers as merely dying vermin, looked upon as despicable dust which no man values, the ruined pivots and pulleys of his rending physical mechanism falling apart, maybe in his mind and heart a far-off vision of the Lake of Galilee and quiet hills and a home of peace whose threshold he shall cross no more, desires to fall asleep on some kind bosom. So, gazing upon the face of Christ, through the thickening gloom, he calls unto him somewhat as a wounded animal caught in the jaws of a steel trap wailingly appeals for help.

Yes, Christ, the object of priestly hatred, the thief saw as the Helper of the helpless. Would that every orphan, every widow, every defeated man, every friendless woman, every despondent soul, every homeless prodigal, could, and would, see him through the eyes of the thief — the **Helper** of the helpless. Would that all men everywhere knew **that** to Jesus there is never a Hill of Difficulty, never a **Valley** of Doubting Castle.

III - THE MOB SAW JESUS AS A MOCK KING AND THE THIEF SAW JESUS AS THE KING OF KINGS.

The hissing mob said: "We have no king but Caesar!" In substance they said: A king? Then a crown he must have. So they crowned him with a crown of thorns. A king? Then the insignia of his high office he needs! So, with the merciless knout, they seamed his quivering flesh until it started up in red scars. A king? Then we must give testimony of our allegiance. So they spat into his face. A king? Then we must raise and reach our hands to him! So they beat him with their fists, slapped him with hard palms, pulled out his beard. A king? Then regal robes he must wear. So they, with studied indignity, put on him a purple robe. A king? Then a scepter he ought to have! So they, in vulgar jest, put a reed in his hand. A king? Then a proclamation must be made! So they bowed the knee in jest and scoffingly said, "Hail, King of the Jews!" A king? Then he ought to have a coronation psalm. So they, with rabble-frenzy, cried out, "Crucify Him!" A king? Then a royal procession he must have! So they led him, as a lamb to the slaughter, to Golgotha. A king? Then he ought to have a throne. So they lifted him upon a wooden cross, himself nailed thereon. A king? Then he ought to have a chalice. So they gave him a sponge filled with vinegar and gall. Mock King!

Not so the thief! He saw Jesus as the Lord who is King forever, the King of Kings, the King of Glory, the everlasting

Ruler of rulers.

Before his crucifixion, after his resurrection, many called Jesus Lord. But only the thief called him Lord as the Potentate of potentates was dying. Socrates had the comradeship of a few loyal friends when he drank the hemlock, but none such had the King of kings when the mob laughed to see him die. Latimer and Ridley, martyrs of old, comforted each other in the flames. But, save the thief, no mouth spoke of Christ's kingdom when, his glory seeming to be in total eclipse, he bled his sweet life away. "Only inanimate nature supplied in her mute elements the sympathy which man denied. Man gazed-readily; the sun refused to look. Man left the crucified naked, but Nature drew a mantle of darkness to hide him from vulgar gaze."

Perhaps — who knows — he had heard the voice of Jesus — months ago. Maybe, sometime, somewhere, he had been one of those who stood upon the edge of the crowd and heard that voice that spoke as never man spake. Maybe — who would deny it? — dim memories of that voice came back to him, echoes of a strange talk about goodness and mercy and — a kingdom. Still the thief gazes upon that face as the midnight shadows come down at noonday. Yes, yes — O God! — this the face that met his somewhere in some place of shame when the Good Shepherd was reaching for his lost sheep. Yes! Yes! — the same strangely radiant face.

And so, at last he speaks. And it is in defense of Christ — it is in rebuke of his evil-minded comrade in crime and in death. And he says: *"Dost not thou fear God, seeing thou art in the same condemnation?"* (Luke 23:40).

Yet the thief saw him as a King worthy our best sacrifice our utmost fealty, our love, our all. The thief saw the kingdom beyond the cross. One asks: "Did not that thief say more in that interview with Christ than some of us have said in our lives? He defended him, hailed him, ascribed to him a kingdom!" "Thy kingdom!" Strange place this to talk of a kindom or kingdoms! A tragic irony!

Oh! I would that all men everywhere would see Jesus

through the eyes of the thief who saw him that dread day
when all furies of hell and all the hatreds of earth assaulted
the King of kings! Would that all would *call* him king, *crown*
him King, *follow* him as King. We mock him when we
remain silent when hostile attacks are made upon him. They
only crown Jesus who obey him. May men see through the
eyes of the thief as they sing:

> "All hail the power of Jesus' name,
>   Let angels prostrate fall!
> Bring forth the royal diadem,
>   And crown him Lord of all!"

IV - THE MOB SAW JESUS AS A SINNER AND THE THIEF SAW JESUS AS A SAVIOUR.

A guilty sinner — dying! A guilty culprit receiving the
just dues of his transgression. "He forbids to pay tribute to
people!" "He is guilty of perverting the nation!" "He made
himself the Son of God!" "We have a law, and by our law he
ought to die!" So they said — accusing him, condemning
him.

But there was one that day who saw him aright. One, a
thief, saw him as he was yesterday, as he is today, as he will
be tomorrow — the sinless Saviour of sinful men. Amid the
triumphs of Christ's enemies and the failure of Christ's
"conquering all the difficulties that sense opposes to its
recognition, saw, even through the dark covering that hid it,
the glory of the Redeemer" — and openly hailed him as
Lord!

A thief! Nothing behind him but the ashes of a wasted
life; nothing before but the fires of an eternal hell! Nothing
behind but the folly of a sinful life; nothing ahead but the
horrors of a sinner's death, Nothing behind but blight;
— the awful outer darkness! Nothing behind but error;
nothing before but terror! Nothing behind but gloom;
nothing ahead but doom; No angels of consolation will
speak his name when he goes shuddering through the gates
of death. Dark, very dark, it will be there. Dreadful,

dreadfully dreadful, it will be there. Lonely, terribly lonely it will be there. So — he puts all his tangled thought into the prayer — "Lord, remember me when thou comest into they kingdom!" The cry it is of an utterly friendless man, a man to whom the loneliness of death is a most tremendous terror.

Yet this thief, seeing him as Saviour, cried out from the depths of a vast abyss: "Lord, remember me when thou comest into thy kingdom!"

But there is another there whose hidden glory bursts through the dark cloud that veiled it. Jesus — able, willing, mighty to save! Jesus — bearing our sins in his own body on the tree! Jesus! He refused the invitation of the mob to come down from the cross — to prove his divinity. And, out of the depths of an infinite love, which no waters can drown, no fires consume, he reaches out to the rescue of the dying thief! Christ Jesus will enter the other world with this poor thief upon his bosom. Shall friend or angel of judgment claim this man's soul when it is Christ who justifies? Nay. Nay — never. For the thief saw him, hailed him as king — as Saviour. Great faith that — blossoming like a lily in a desert! Wonderful faith that — giving forth fragrance like a full-blown rose in a garbage can!

Oh! That all sin-doomed, sin-damned, sin-blighted, sin-cursed, sin-ruined, sin-scarred, sin-marred sinners everywhere could see, and would see Jesus through the eyes of that thief. Then they would find entrance into the Paradise of God. Then they would pray, even as now we pray:

"Carry me over the long, last mile,
  Man of Nazareth, Christ for me.
Weary I wait at Death's dark stile,
  And the wild and the waste, where the winds blow free
And the shadows and sorrows come out of my past,
  Look keen through my heart
  And will not depart,

Now that my poor world has come to its last!

"Lord, is it long that my spirit must wait,
   Man of Nazareth, Christ for me?
Deep is the stream, and the night is late,
   And grief blinds my soul that I cannot see.
Speak to me out of the silences, Lord,
   That my spirit may know,
   As I forward go,
That Thy pierced hands are lifting me over the
ford!"

IT IS FINISHED

"It is finished" — John 19:30

7

Jesus, on Golgotha, looked up and down.

He looked up to God and thought of his having glorified his name, having finished the work that God gave him to do. — He looked down to men and thought of the saving power which his cross was to exert over millions of the human family.

And it was a moment of intensest joy — his last pang endured, his last service rendered, his vicarious work completed.

And he said, "It is finished." That expression is the authoritative chronicle of sacrificial redemption. That is the meaning of the text, and the only meaning. Let us fasten the microscopes of spiritual scrutiny and the telescopes of spiritual observation upon this text — one of the greatest in all the Bible — and pray that, in what we shall say, we shall not spoil God's fair lilies with man's mean paint!

I - A CRY OF JOY, OF SUPREME SATISFACTION, OVER A FINISHED WORK.

The more difficult and prolonged any task is, the greater is the satisfaction in finishing it. Every one who has aimed at the best, and has worked nobly to achieve the best, knows what it means, after accomplishing anything on which a great deal of labor has been bestowed or the accomplishment of which has been delayed, to be able to say, "There, it is finished at last!"

As Gray — after finishing his elegy, every line of which is like a jewel falling down a golden stairway. As Virgil — after finishing his "Aeneid," all of which is most masterful. As Palissy — after working sixteen years, amid poverty and trial in toil and suffering, to find the secret of white enamel. As Goodyear — after working eleven years for the secret of vulcanizing rubber, no one believing him the while but his wife. As Morse — when, amid the adverse criticisms of the press and the jeers of Congress, the metallic lips of his telegraph instrument startled the world with the words, "What hath God wrought?" As Cyrus Field — when after thirty different attempts covering a period of ten years, during which time his cable was denounced as a mad freak of stubborn ignorance, he put it into the ocean bed and it began to quiver with the news of the world. As McCormick — when, amid jeers and ridicule that tried his soul as fire, he got his reaper finished — a machine that moved all the nations of the world out of the bread line. As Galileo — when he finished the telescope which brought the worlds and the stars nearer to man's eye. As Bell — when, after being called a mad man at the Centennial Exposition in 1876, he transmitted the human voice across the continent by means of wires. As the builder of Taj Mahal — when, after 20,000 men worked on it for twenty years, was able to say, "It is finished!" As Solomon — when, after 180,000 men had worked on it for seven and one-half years, he could say, "The glorious temple is finished!"

And others!

In the more signal efforts of human genius and energy, there is a satisfaction in final achievement which warms even spectators to admiration and praise across the space of hundreds of years.

What must it be to the poet, after equipping himself by the labors of a lifetime, with the stores of knowledge and the skill required in the use of language for the composition of a "Divine Comedy" or a "Paradise Lost," and after wearing himself lean for many years at the task, to be able, penning the last line, to say with satisfaction, "It is finished!"

What must it have been to Columbus, after he had worn his life out in seeking the patronage necessary for his undertaking, and having endured the perils of voyaging across unchartered seas and among mutinous mariners, to see, at last, the sunlight on the peak of Darien — which light informed him that his dream was true and his life work accomplished?

When we read how William Wilberforce, the champion of slave emancipation, heard, on his death-bed, that the British Legislature had agreed to the expenditure necessary to secure the object to which he had sacrificed his life — what heart can refuse its sympathetic joy, as it thinks of him expiring with the shouts of emancipated millions in his ears?

These are but feeble and faint suggestions of that which Christ saw, fallen behind, his task accomplished, as he cried, "It is finished!" Over his teaching, he had satisfaction — wonderful satisfaction. Over his life, he had satisfaction — sweet satisfaction. Over his miracles, he had satisfaction — comforting satisfaction.

But the satisfaction of these could not compare with the satisfaction which was his, when amid the low shame and sore torment of the Cross, he cried with inarticulate loud voice and then, in an articulate voice, saying "It is finished!"

Because he had something in his mind greater than his teachings. Greater than his life itself. Greater than his miracles. Which brings us to the question — what was finished?

We answer that in part when we say

II - THAT CRY — "IT IS FINISHED" — WAS A DEATH-KNELL.

A death-blow? Yes, a death knell? Yes. But — a death-blow to what? A death-blow — a finishing of — the dispensation of types and symbols.

Adam was a type of Christ because he came directly from God.

Melchisedek was a type of Christ because he was without beginning, without end.

Isaac was a type of Christ because he was offered on the altar of sacrifice.

Moses was a type of Christ because he was a great emancipator.

Joseph was a type of Christ in that he was despised by his brethren.

Solomon — because of the affluence of his reign.

Joshua — because of his victorious conquests.

Samson — because he carried off the gates of impossibility.

- Jonah was a type of Christ because he was thrown into the midst of the sea to save others from distress.

- All these were types of Christ in some special application.

Noah's ark, the rent veil, the ark of the covenant, the mercy seat, the brazen altar, the golden altar, the golden candle stick, the brazen laver, the manna, the brazen serpent, the Rock of Horeb, the cities of refuge, the tree of life — all, in some sense, types of Christ — and are so treated in the Scriptures.

So the High Priest of the Jews, in the performance of every function appertaining to his sacerdotal office, was a type of Christ our High Priest — especially and preeminently so when on the great annual day of Atonement he went into the Holy of holies and sprinkled the blood seven times upon the mercy seat, and seven times before it.

So the High Priest stood before the ark — typical of Christ — clothed in robes, typical of Christ's righteousness. Upon his bosom his breastplate with twelve precious stones severally engraved with the names of the twelve tribes of Israel — typical of the abiding interest of all the Israel of God in the mediation of Christ — typical in expressing the truth that their names are imperishably engraven upon Christ's memory and heart.

"In the breastplate the Urim and Thummin — Urim signifying lights, Thummin signifying perfection — in virtue of which the priest gave oracular answers to the people — typical that God through Christ is the source of all experimentally religious knowledge, and the infallible truth of salvation's plan as accomplished by the work of Christ and taught by his sacred lips — and by the lips of others.

"Upon his brow a golden mitre engraved with the phrase 'Holiness unto the Lord' — typically testifying that perfect holiness was essential in a mediator between God and man — typically testifying that the coming Saviour would possess the required qualifications."

In his hand a censer of burning incense — typical of the intercessions of Christ and of God's great pleasure in a reconciliation with man through Christ.

This High Priest stood sprinkling blood, the instrument of propitiation with man through Christ.

The throne, the symbol of being to be propitiated.

All typical of the expiatory nature and efficency of the blood of Christ.

The High Priest sprinkled the propitiatory blood upon the mercy seat, and before the mercy seat seven times — seven meaning perfection — typical of the perfect atonement to be made by Christ.

God instituted this sacrificial worship as typical.

Every sacrifice made before the Flood, every sacrifice

offered during the days of the patriarchs, every sacrifice offered by the Jews during all the years of Judaism — all were a type of Christ.

The crooked smoke that arose from Abel's altar, and the smoke from all the altars of Abraham and Noah and from the altars of the more diversified and systematic sacrifices of the Jews, gave evidence that the people were looking away by faith to the promised Seed, even Jesus.

Like finger-posts along the dusty highway of Time, they pointed the faith of the worshipers to a sacrificial Saviour.

Types, they foreshadowed the great ANTI-TYPE. Adumbrations of a substance yet to come, significant shadows of redemptive entity still ahead, preparing and opening the way for something better through the rites imposing, through symbols splendid, through services sublime, these sacrifices were not ultimate but introductory.

The finishing of Christ's redemptive work on the Cross was the finishing of all these.

"It is finished," said Christ. And the vast system of the patriarchs and Judaism, colossal in structure, hoary in antiquity, passed away. Far into oblivion its altars, dripping with blood, drifted. For centuries, in shattered shreds upon the ruins of history, its priestly vestments have been flung.

Jesus, the great ANTI-TYPE took all its rites, types, symbols, with him to the Cross, and nailed them there. They died with him. They were buried with him. He rose. They did not. *"Nailed to the cross"* (Col. 2:14).

"The veil of the temple was rent in twain from the top to the bottom" (Matt. 27:51).

Meaning what? Meaning this: The Holy of holies in the Son of man is revealed. His altars are now manifest to all. In his salvation there are no priestly secrets. A child can learn his oracles. The old priesthood is superseded; the old sacrifices have lost their value and are absorbed in the one great sacrifice for sin. And because this one great sacrifice for sin, Jesus being both High Priest and Lamb of God, we say:

"But beloved, we are persuaded better things of you, and things that accompany salvation" (Hebrew 6:9).

"Having therefore, brethren, boldness to enter into the holiest by the blood of Jesus" (Hebrew 10:19).

"And from Jesus Christ, who is the faithful witness, and the first begotten of the dead, and the prince of the kings of the earth. Unto him that loved us, and washed us from our sins in his own blood, and hath made us kings and priests unto God and his Father; to him be glory and dominion for ever and ever. Amen" (Rev. 1:5-6).

The types were redemption symbolized. The Christ redemption realized.

Yes, the ceremonial law with its mystic rites and interposed barriers was abrogated. The mercy seat, and the ark of the covenant with the broken tables of the law, and the pot of manna lay within the Holy of holies. Now they stood revealed. Better still, they were charged with new meaning as these symbols were interpreted in the light of Christ's redemption. Henceforth the way to the Mercy Seat lay not through the sacrifice offered by human hands, but through the Lamb himself.

All pointed to Jesus. Daniel tells when Christ will come. Micah where he will come from; Malachi of his forerunner. The Old Testament began with Christ, and it ends with him. "The testimony of Jesus is the spirit of prophecy," says John. Jesus is the Alpha and Omega of the Bible, its animus, its mind, its spirit the anti-type of its types. He is the vital substance which gives meaning to its genealogies, meaning to its histories, meaning to its chronologies; the secret of its unity; the secret of its strength; the secret of its beauty."

III - THE DEBT OF SIN IS PAID.

"It is finished."

The reality of sin and its deadly power makes the gravest problem with which human thought has ever grappled. Man in debt. Can't pay out.

"Put that to mine account." That is "It is finished," in

other words!

By every thorn that punctured his brow, by every pang of pain, by every nail which pierced him, by the savage Roman spear that drank from his side the precious libation of blood and water, by every drop of sinless blood shed that day, he said "the debt is paid."

The debt paid — not with corruptible things such as silver and gold, from our vain manner of life handed down from our fathers, but with precious blood, as a Lamb without blemish and without spot, even the blood of Jesus! Christ paid the tribute money. There is exemption. There is redemption.

"It is finished." There is nothing further when everything is finished. Ripened the fruit of the truth that he was made under the law to redeem them that are under the law.

God has fully dealt for us with the law's claims that man shall deserve acceptance. Legal satisfaction is forever taken out of our hands by Christ. Christ himself dealt, in the sinner's interest, with the law, honoring its holy claims to the uttermost under the human conditions which he freely undertook, so that, by faith the community between Jesus and the sinner is real, the community of the sinner's debt on one side and Christ's merit on the other side.

The believer is complete in him. The believer's hand is free because Christ's was crushed. The believer's brow is painless now because Christ's was bound. The believer's soul escapes because Christ's was bound. The believer gains heaven because Christ, for the believer, endured the torture and went through the horrors of hell. All the weapons of eternal wrath struck him, but as they struck him our race marched out free — from debt.

"By his stripes we are healed." He died, not for his own sins, but for ours. He had no sin in him. He humbled himself that we might be exalted. He became poor that we might become rich. He was wounded that we might be healed. He drained the cup of wrath that we might drink the water of salvation. For us and to pay our debt he came into the midst of earth's night to give us light, into the midst of earth's sorrows to give joy, into the midst of earth's storm to give calm; into the midst of earth's death to give life; into the midst of earth's bondage to give liberty.

"Put that to mine account." Jesus paid the debt. God is just. And he will not demand two payments for one debt. No. No honest man will demand two payments for one debt. No honest banker will demand two payments for one debt. Therefore, when I trust him, my debt is paid. All of it is paid!

> "Jesus paid it all,
>   All to him I owe;
> Sin had left a crimson stain,
>   He washed it white as snow!"

Every legal and philosophical condition involved in the nature of God, his attributes, system, government, law, in the nature of man, in man's relations and conditions and in the nature of things necessary to a perfect redemption, was fully met in the nature, character, work, sufferings, and death of Jesus!

> "My sins laid open to the rod,
>   The back which from the law was free,
> And the Eternal Son of God,
>   Received the stripes once due to me!

> "I pierced those sacred hands and feet
>   That never touched or walked in sin,
> I broke the heart that only beat,
>   The souls of sinful men to win!

> "No beam was in his eye or mote,
>   Nor laid to him was any blame,
> And yet his cheeks for me were smote,
>   The cheeks that never blushed for shame!
> "The sponge of vinegar and gall

By me was placed under his tongue
And when derision mocked his call,
I stood that mocking crowd among.

"And yet his blood was shed for me,
To be of sin the double cure,
And balm there flows from Calvary's tree,
That heals my guilt and makes me pure!"

For every drunkard who will trust he says, "Put that to my account." For every liar, for every thief, for every adulterer, for every murderer he says, "Put that to mine account." There is exemption and there is redemption. There is nothing for us to do but to accept it through faith! But we must accept it. All the ceremonial sacrifices could not obtain the bond from the hand of the creditor. They were only acknowledgment of the debt. Jesus, by one offering, paid the whole, took up the bond, the handwriting that was against us, and nailed it to the Cross. And, when driving the last nail, he cried, "It is finished!"

The statement — "It is finished" — means

IV - THE SHADOW OF THE CROSS LIFTED FROM JESUS.

Earth has no darker sin, history no blacker page, humanity has no fouler spot than that of the Saviour's crucifixion.

Jesus was born with the mark of the Cross upon his shoulders. With the weight of the Cross upon his heart, he learned to walk. With the weight of the Cross upon his shoulders, he learned to work. He bowed to baptism with the weight of the Cross upon him. He endured temptation with the weight of the Cross upon him. He began his ministry with the weight of the Cross upon him. From his earliest moment it was his burden by day, his pallet by night. From Bethlehem into Egypt, with the shadow of the Cross upon him, he went. He climbed Olivet oppressed by its weight. He walked the streets dishonored by its shame. He rose from the dead glorified by its sacrifice.

The Cross was with him when they came with their lanterns and torches seeking the Light of the World. The Cross was with him when Judas, with a kiss that burned his cheek like a hot sword, betrayed him. The Cross was with him when Annas asked him concerning his disciples and doctrine. The Cross was with him when Caiaphas condemned him. The Cross was with him when Herod mocked him. The Cross was with him when the people derided him.

"The shadow of the Cross was on Bethlehem's swaddling clothes. The shadow of the Cross was on the road to Egypt. The shadow of the Cross was on opal and amethyst and emerald floor by Lake Galilee. The shadow of the cross was on the door of the Temple. The shadow of the Cross was on the sunrise and sunset."

But now the shadow of the Cross is lifted. Never again shall he be persecuted from city to city, called a glutton and winebibber and a bastard and servant of Satan. Never again shall he sweat blood. Never again shall he say, "My soul is exceeding sorrowful unto death," and then go forth to a garden where the roots of his divine emotion put forth their crimson tears. Never again shall he be derided by the rabble. Never again shall be be spit upon and slapped and buffeted. Never again shall he be crowned with thorns. Never again shall he be lacerated with the scourge. Never again will he cry out in the anguish of his soul, "My God, my God, why has thou forsaken me?"

On every path he walked, on every house he entered, on every city he visited was the shadow of the Cross which now, because of his death, is lifted.

V - WHAT WAS FINISHED?

"It is finished!"

What was finished? Something has been accomplished. He hath finished the transgression and made reconciliation for iniquity, and brought in everlasting righteousness and sealed up the vision and the prophecy, and anointed a Holy of holies!

The long list of prophecies beginning with Genesis 3:6, the Jewish economy of types and rituals, the work the Father had given him to do, the matchless beauty of a perfect life, the claims of a broken law. All were finished. Eternal justice was satisfied, righteousness vindicated, and heaven's throne established.

"mercy and truth are met together; righteousness and peace have kissed each other" (Psalms 85:10).

Man's redemption is secured, and nothing left undone for man to do but to accept, receive, rejoice!

"It is finished!" At the transfiguration they spoke of a death which he would accomplish at Jerusalem. He has now reached the finishing touch. It is finished. Redemption is an accomplished fact.

There is no more to be done. This God-Man when he had made one sacrifice for sins forever, sat down at the right hand of God.

The types are now all full.

The Old Testament pictures are now fulfilled. No more blood of bulls and goats on Jewish altars slain, no more burnt-offering meal-offering, peace-offering, trespass-offering, sin-offerings. "By one offering he hath perfected forever."

No more lambs led to the slaughter, no more bullocks bound with cords in the horns of the altar of burnt offering, no more goats carried to the land of forgetfulness. No more shadows henceforth and forever.

When beginning his ministry he said: "I must be about my Father's business." Now he hath finished the transaction, and soon he will proclaim his triumph.

His meat was to do the will of God, which will he hath done. It is finished. When work is done, rest follows. Why not accept the finished work and forever cease, save from the work which is sweet service to him, whose sacrifice hath made thee whole?

What was finished? Redemption's completion! There it stood. The study of angels. The hope of men. The wonder of the universe. The crowning work of creation's God. The masterpiece of heaven! Finished!

What was finished? The abolishment of death as a penalty for every believer. True, the Christian dies. But his death is no longer penal, but providential and provisional.

What was finished? The atonement fundamental to salvation is accomplished. As the bridge is fundamental to span the river, the foundation fundamental to the building, the blood fundamental to the body, the rails fundamental to the train, the mould fundamental to the pattern, the power fundamental to the car, that graft fundamental to alter the fruit, so the death of Christ's atonement is fundamental to bring us to God — to rest our conscience in peace, to cause the life to function in the will of God, to keep our lives along the line of sacrifice, to mould us to die in the pattern of his sacrificial service, and to produce the fruit unto holiness in the spirit of him who loved us and gave himself for us.

What was finished? The guilt and demerit of sin which induced the penalty of death have been set aside for all for whom the substitution avails. That is finished.

What was finished? The law that was hidden in his heart, as it was hidden in the ark of the covenant, was fulfilled to the letter. It was that complete fulfillment which found its accent in his cry on the Cross, "It is finished."

What was finished? Christ's intercourse with his disciples? No, for it was to be continued through forty wonderful days. Christ's preaching the word of life? No, for that was continued through the disciples who were to carry the gospel to the ends of the earth. What then was finished, if not these things?

The great mission on which our Lord came to earth was finished, that for which the Son of God took on our human form and lived among men and died at last on the Cross — that was finished in the atonement for our sins. Finished was the age-long plan of salvation. Sacrificed finally was the

Lamb slain by anticipation from the foundation of the world. Completed was God's sacrificial purpose for his creatures. Finished the proof and standing evidence of divine love, held up forever, nailed to the bloody Cross!

Well might Jesus cry, "It is finished!" And now let every grateful life respond "In my heart and in my life it is begun!"

What was finished? His "gory crown was changed to a glory crown." May we not say that that which brought the gory was the glory? If there had been no gory crown, there could have been no glory crown.

What was finished? God's announcement by the voice of the prophets that the old covenant was obliterated and abrogated and that a new covenant was here. The blood of animals sprinkled upon stubborn heads, upon blaspheming faces, had lost its virtue — another blood, pure and precious, was "drawn from Immanuel's veins."

What was finished? The hour for which he came into the world had run its course. The cup which with such a trembling hand he had put to shrinking lips has been drunk to its dregs. The powers of darkness have made on him, amid furies of earth and the hatreds of hell their last assault — and though darkness knew it not, have been repelled. Their momentary darkness of the Father's countenance has passed away.

What was finished? "Tis done, the great transaction is done." The perfect fulfillment of all the law required is finished.

What was finished? There was finished upon the Cross the new, the full, the wonderful revelation of the Father, that unbosoming of the Eternal, the opening up to us of the very heart of the Godhead, the exhibition of the mingled love and holiness of our Father who is in heaven. There was completed then that glorious, that attractive, that subduing manifestation of the love of God for sinful men, which carried the divine being to the extreme length of suffering and of self-sacrifice, and which has ever formed the most powerful of all instruments of pacifying the conscience, melting the heart, moulding the character, renewing and sanctifying the will.

What was finished? Whatever obstacles our guilt threw in the way of our being received back into the divine favor, have been removed. Whatever the integrity of his law, and the moral interests of his government required in the way of atonement or expiation, has been rendered. The way of access to God is lying quite open to us. That is what was meant when Jesus said: "It is finished." amid the darkness and blood of Calvary's hill. That is what is meant now when, amid the quiet of our homes, we read the story of the Cross. All our guilt is buried, buried beyond being raised again in the depths of his atonement.

Finished! It seemed the finishing of him — an inglorious defeat. Three years of ministry. A bribed disciple. An arrest at midnight. Pilate washing his hands of guilty blood. A cross swaying in the darkness with a white blood-splotched naked body upon it, and an earthquake, and a BURIAL.

But, at last, human history unrolls its vast scroll! The scene is ablaze with light. The voice of the prophets swell into thunder-peals of triumph. Mount Sinai kneels before Calvary. The Occident takes the place of the Orient in the march of the ages, and revolutions and reformations of twenty centuries, the wonders of modern civilization, attesting the glories of his triumphs. King — all hail! "WONDERFUL!"

United States history records the building of a great transcontinental railway line which would unite the country by rail from the Atlantic to the Pacific.

During the construction financial embarrassment overtook the promoters, and with difficulty they secured the funds. There was rejoicing when the work was resumed. The day came when the last rail was set on the border line between New Mexico and Colorado. It was planned to be a great event. A special order was sent to California for a laurel wood tie, and two silver spikes were ordered — one for Colorado and one for New Mexico. The Governor of each State was invited. They were to drive the two silver spikes into the laurel wood tie, thus completing the work of construction, making a way of transportation from ocean to ocean and binding together the two states.

As the Governors drove the two silver spikes into the laurel wood tie, the great crowd applauded, and a tapped telegraph wire bore the news with a flash out to the entire country and the world! It was a great feat and accomplishment.

There was a day when four spikes were driven, not into a laurel tie, but into a cursed tree and through the hands and feet of the Son of God!

They were not spikes of silver, but of iron and steel and driven while heaven, earth, and underneath looked on. Then the last spike was driven, a shout went up from all the creation — the news flashed to the end of the world for a way of transportation from sin and its darkness has been completed! "It is finished" was the cry!

The way was now open from earth to heaven! There was a trail to the end! A means of access to God had been completed! The spikes were not driven by friends, but by enemies, for it was while we were yet enemies, Christ died for us! The last spike driven through the hands of the Son of God on the rugged Cross brought man and God together! It was a reconciling death! It was a peace-making transaction. The bonded indebtedness was now fully met and the debt was paid.

It was one certain day in the reign of Tiberius that the bond fell due. The Holy One and the Just One came forward in surety and cried "Set that to mine account." He climbed that Cross, that cursed tree, with an unforced will! He yielded his hands to those spikes of iron. From the spike of iron came forth the "rod of iron" with which he will yet rule the nations! "O glorious transaction, 'tis done!" Shout it forth, cry aloud, the way to God is an open way! "It is finished!"

GOD'S BEST-DRESSED MAN

TEXT:
"and thou shalt make holy garments for Aaron thy brother for glory and for beauty" (Exodus 28:2).

Dr. Frank S. Mead writes this about Aaron:

"The magic sand of greatness never touched the shoulder of Aaron. Older than Moses in years, he was younger in genius and character.

In Egypt he was his brother's mouthpiece, the bumper between the elders and the people, between Pharaoh and Israel as well. He did the talking.

He also did the praying. He was the senior member of that distinguished clan of high-priests of Levi which held sway over Israel for sixteen hundred years. He was the instrument of most of the Exodus miracles. He loved God.

He was eloquent but unstable; witness his erection of the golden calf and his ridiculous explanation. He was weak in danger and irresolute; witness his willingness to let Miriam take the whole blame for their foolhardy little rebellion. He was strong so long as he had Moses to lean upon. But when left to himself he was quite apt to fail. Such men are valuable, but we cannot trust them far.

His life is a study in chaos. Promise and uncertainty fought for him. Uncertainty won. He died in disgrace, stripped of his priestly robe and office.

The mind of Moses dominated him and left him weak."

But more interesting and spiritually significant is what was done by Moses, under the command of God, in dressing his brother in holy garments of glory and beauty.

Note the specific directions God gave as to certain people.

"And thou shalt speak unto all that are wise hearted, whom I have filled with the spirit of wisdom, that they may make Aaron's garments to consecrate him, that he may minister unto me in the priest's office" (Exodus 28:3).

Holy garments.
Garments of glory.
Garments of beauty.
What about these garments?
God tells us:

"And these are the garments which they shall make; a breastplate, and an ephod, and a robe, and a broidered coat, a mitre, and a girdle: and they shall make holy garments for Aaron thy brother, and his sons, that he may minister unto me in the priest's office" (Exodus 28:4)

Truly, Aaron was a God-clothed man. And in this act of God-designed decoration, we behold our Lord Jesus Christ in typical prefiguration — as many truth lovers and expositors of the Word have made known to us.

Moses, doing what God commanded him to do, dressed Aaron in the eight holy garments of glory and beauty. He put them on Aaron piece by piece — so that they could be seen in all the details of skilled workmanship and surpassing beauty. On Aaron was put the embroidered linen coat with the linen breeches. He was girdled with the girdle which bound him in with its fineness of texture and perfection of color.

Moses put on Aaron the blue robe with its ringing golden bells and pomgranates in their trinity of color. Moses put on the gold ephod, buttoned it on the shoulders with two onyx stones, set the breast plate, and put on the Urim and Thummin — two precious stones signifying light and perfection. Then this was bound to the shoulders with wreathen chains, underneath the ephod at the waist with the curious girdle or belt.

Last of all, Moses took the snowy white linen, wound it fold on fold around his head, making a turban of it. Then he put blue lace on the front of it, and on that fastened the golden plate with the graven words upon it — "Holiness to the Lord." In this manner of investiture, the people saw the intricate worth of these garments of glory and beauty. Thus they beheld Aaron set apart from all others — exalted above the people, yet for the people.

Let us consider first the

I - BREASTPLATE

The Bible describes it in detail. The details are somewhat bewildering:

"And thou shalt make the breastplate of judgment with cunning work; after the work of the ephod thou shalt make it; of gold, of blue, and of purple, and of scarlet, and of fine twined linen, shalt thou

make it. Foursquare it shall be being doubled; a span shall be the length thereof, and a span shall be the breadth thereof. And thou shalt set in it settings of stones, even four rows of stones: the first row shall be a sardius, a topaz, and a carbuncle: this shall be the first row. And the second row shall be an emerald, a sapphire, and a diamond. And the third row a ligure, an agate, and an amethyst. And the fourth row a beryl, and an onyx, and a jasper: they shall be set in gold in their inclosings. And the stones shall be with the names of the children of Israel, twelve, according to their names, like the engravings of a signet; every one with his name shall they be according to the twelve tribes. And thou shalt make upon the breastplate chains at the ends of wreathen work of pure gold. And thou shalt make upon the breastplate two rings of gold, and shalt put the two rings on the two ends of the breastplate. And thou shalt put the two wreathen chains of gold in the two rings which are on the ends of the breastplate" (Exodus 28:15-24).

What does this breastplate signify?

Christ when He had glory with God before the world was and was loved by the Father before the foundation of the world (John 17) — when, in Eternity, He rested on the bosom of the Father without an earthly mother — just as when, in Time, He rested on the bosom of a mother without an earthly father.

Jesus said: *"The Father and I are one"* (John 10:30) — and *"God is love"* (I John 3:16).

He was a LOVING Christ when He worked in the carpenter shop in Nazareth.

He was a LOVING Christ when "He went about doing good" — working miracles of healing.

He was the LOVING Christ when, in blazing, righteous anger, He drove the money-greedy, money-grabbing hucksters from the Father's house, which these men had made "a den of thieves" instead of a house of prayer (Matt. 21:12-13).

He was the LOVING Christ when, in teaching, He spoke as never man spoke — *"as one having authority and not as the scribes and Pharisees"* (Matt. 7:29).

He was the LOVING Christ when He chose His twelve disciples and sent them forth to proclaim to others the truths of His gospel.

He was the LOVING Christ when He observed the Passover for the last time and instituted the Lord's Supper in the Upper Room.

He was the LOVING Christ when, in Gethsemane's garden, He did sweat blood — as our sins walked with hobnail boots on His tender heart.

He was the LOVING Christ when He was arrested, buffeted, bruised and led forth to die on the horrible Roman cross.

He was the LOVING Christ when on that cross He saved the dying thief and willed His mother to John, the Apostle.

He was the LOVING Christ when, rising from the dead, He smashed at one blow Death's empire of skulls and skeletons and *"showed Himself alive by many infallible proofs"* (Acts 1:3).

He was the LOVING Christ when, marred and scarred, with the stigmata of the Cross, He, with clouds as His chariot and the wind as His steeds, went back to the Father's right hand — where He ever liveth to make intercession for us and from whence He shall return in the air and a little later to the earth.

Since the BREASTPLATE signifies the Christ who was the Christ of LOVE in all places and at all times, the truth should urge us to live lives of love — giving heed to what the Apostle Paul wrote:

"But as touching brotherly love ye need not that I write unto you: for ye yourselves are taught of God to

love one another. And indeed ye do it toward all the brethren which are in all Macedonia: but we beseech you, brethren, that ye increase more and more;" (I Thess. 4:9-10).

- Now note:

II - THE EPHOD

"And they shall take gold, and blue, and purple, and scarlet, and fine twined linen, with cunning work" (Exodus 28:5-6).

It was held together front and back by two shoulder pieces at the top and a girdle band around the waist. On each shoulder piece was an onyx stone engraven with six names of the tribes of Israel.

This EPHOD speaks of the human and divine Christ.

Son of man was Christ. Son of God was Christ. And both in one.

As man He got tired; as God, He said, *"Come unto me, all ye that labour and are heavy laden, and I will give you rest"* (Matt. 11:28).

As man, He got hungry; as God, He fed thousands with a lad's lunch (John 6:9).

As man, He got thirsty; as God, He gave living water (John 4:10).

As man, He prayed; as God, He made, in praying no confession of sin.

As man, He was tempted in all points like as we are; as God, He was without sin, baffling His enemies with the question, *"Who convinceth Me of sin?"* (John 8:46).

As man, He slept; as God, He arose from sleep and stilled the raging tempest.

As man, He sorrowed over separation from friends; as God, He promised never to leave them comfortless, and to come to them (John 14:1).

As man, a ship carried Him; as God, He walked on the

rolling, tumbling sea (John 6:19).

As man, He accepted a village girl's invitation to her wedding; as God, He there changed water into wine.

As man, He was despised of men; as God, *"all the angels of God worship Him"* (Heb. 1:6).

As man, He got lonely; as God, He said, *"The Father hath not left me alone"* (John 9:29).

As man, He longed for human companionship and sympathy; as God, He *"trod the wine-press alone"* (Isa. 63:3).

As man, He wept at Lazarus' grave; as God, He raised Lazarus from the dead.

As man, He grew in wisdom and stature; as God, *"He upholdeth all things by the word of His power"* (Hebrews 1:3).

Give thought now to the

III - ROBE

"And thou shalt make the robe of the ephod all of blue. And there shall be an hole in the top of it, in the midst thereof: it shall have a binding of woven work round about the hole of it, as it were the hole of an habergeon, that it not be rent. And beneath upon the hem of it thou shalt make pomegranates of blue, and of purple, and of scarlet, round about the hem thereof; and bells of gold between them round about. A golden bell and a pomegranate, a golden bell and a pomegranate, upon the hem of the robe round about" (Exodus 28:31-34).

That garment of glory and beauty speaks of the heavenly and gracious Christ.

Yes — the great Unlike.

Yes — the One superlatively unique.

John the Baptist said: *"He that cometh from above is above all: he that is of the earth is earthly, and speaketh of the earth: he that cometh from heaven is above all"* (John 3:31).

The enemies of Jesus said: *"Our fathers did eat manna in the desert; as it is written, He gave them bread from heaven to eat"* (John 6:31).

Jesus, answering them, said:

"Then Jesus said unto them, Verily, verily, I say unto you, Moses gave you not that bread from heaven; but my Father giveth you the true bread from heaven. For the bread of God is he which cometh down from heaven, and giveth life unto the world" (John 6:32-33).

The Jews, malicious in their attitude toward Jesus, murmured against him, because He said: *"I am the Bread which cometh down from heaven"* (John 6:41).

Jesus said: *"I am the living bread which came down from heaven: if any man eat of this bread, he shall live forever: and the bread that I will give is my flesh, which I will give for the life of the world"* (John 6:58).

And *"This is that bread which came down from heaven: not as your fathers did eat manna, and are dead: he that eateth of this bread shall live forever"* (John 6:58).

And this wonderful Christ Jesus cannot be fully described and delineated. The world over, architects, striving to build cathedrals worthy of him, fall short of their high objectives. Painters, vieing with painters, feel incompetent to create figures beautiful enough to adorn his sanctuary walls. A sense of inadequacy falls oppressively upon musicians who try to create music sweet enough for his hymns of praise. Sculptors, searching all quarries, nowhere can find marble white enough for his forehead. Orators, whose sentences are flights of golden arrows, express only a meager measure of the honor due him. Writers, words dropping from their pens like golden pollen from stems of shaken lilies, feel the inadequacy of all words to set him forth in his beauty. Devout poets, reaching from pole to pole with the wings of their poetic genius, struggle for some metaphor with which to express him. Profound scholars, rushing with archangelic splendor through mysterious realms of thought, light their brightest torches at his altar fires.

"No mortal can with him compare,
Among the sons of men
Fairer is he than all the fair
Who fill the heavenly train."

Give thought now to the

IV - LINEN COAT AND BREECHES

These set forth the truth of the SINLESS Christ. *"He knew no sin"* (II Cor. 5:21).

Jesus, in verbal warfare with the religionists and the hypocrites of His day, made some statements and asked a question:

"Ye are of your father the devil and the lusts of your father ye will do. He was a murderer from the beginning, and abode not in the truth, because there is no truth in him. When he speaketh a lie, he speaketh of his own: for he is a liar, and the father of it. And because I tell you the truth, ye believe me not. Which of you convinceth me of sin? And if I say the truth, why do ye not believe me?" (John 8:44-46).

The sinless Christ was Jesus of Nazareth. He was so finely strung, so unutterably keyed to truth, and mercy and justice and love and so quickly felt the sorrow, the sympathy, and the indignation which wrong and injustice invariably elicit from all high souls.

Circumstances never left their finger prints upon His character. Popularity never caused Him to falter or to fear the revilings of men. Though tempted in all points like as we are (Hebrews 4:15), though He Himself *"suffered being tempted"* (Heb. 2:18), though *"Jesus was led of the Spirit into the wilderness to be tempted of the Devil"* (Matt. 4:4), temptations never loosened a moral fibre. Though He was moneyless and had no pocketbook but the mouth of a fish, though the foxes had holes and the birds of the air had nests for home, and He, as Son of Man, had nowhere to lay His head (Matt. 5:20), He never worried about money matters.

Never was He unjust to any man. Never was He indiscreet or condemnatory as to any woman. Never was He unkind to any little child. He sought no crown or throne from men.

We read: *"When Jesus therefore perceived that they would come and take him by force, to make him a king, he departed again into a mountain himself alone"* (John 6:15). Never did He have fear of any tyrant or wicked ruler.

The world agrees with the judgment of poltroomic Pilate who said: *"I find no fault in Him"* (John 18:38). And with Pilate's wife who wrote her husband, *"Have nothing to do with this just man"* (Matt. 27:19). And with Judas who said: *"I have betrayed THE innocent blood"* (Matt. 27:14). And with the centurion who supervised the bloody-butchery of the crucifixion and who, seeing the sinless Christ die, said: *"Surely, this man was the Son of God"* (Matt. 27:54). And with God who said: *"This is my beloved Son in whom I am well-pleased"* (Matt. 3:17). And Christ Himself who said: *"He that sent me is with me: the Father hath not left me alone: for I do always those things that please him"* (John 8:29).

And now give thought to the

V - GIRDLE

It is spoken of as *"the curious girdle of the ephod"* (Exodus 28:27). *"And they shall bind the breastplate by the rings thereof unto the rings of the ephod with a lace of blue, that it may be above the curious girdle of the ephod, and that the breastplate be not loosed from the ephod"* (Exodus

28:28).

The girdle speaks of the SERVING Christ. Jesus was the servant of God — and of man. *"He took upon Himself the form of a servant "* (Phil. 2:7). So testified Paul — by the Holy Spirit.

And Jesus said:

"But it shall not be so among you: but whosoever will be great among you, let him be your minister; and whosoever will be chief among you, let him be your servant: Even as the Son of man came not to be ministered unto, but to minister, and to give his life a ransom for many" (Matt. 20:26-28).

"But so shall it not be among you: but whosoever will be great among you, shall be your minister" (Mark 10:43).

Paul said: *"I have made myself a servant to all"* (I Cor. 9:19).

In that spirit of Jesus that possessed Paul, he became GREAT. He compassed the earth with the truth of Gospel redemption. He put out the altar fires of Diana. He lit a Gospel lamp in the palace of the Caesars. He stormed the capitals of proud empires in the name of Jesus.

CHRIST the greatest of the great, the one wonderful UNIQUE, was a SERVANT. And we should seek to be GREAT by rendering SERVICE — by being servants. He who would be great among you, let him be rich, let him be high educated, let him be talented, let him be musical, let him be a great athlete, let him be a holder of high political office. NO! "Let him be servant."

Frank Crane said about Lincoln: "He was not a ruler — as Julius Caesar. He was one of the greatest SERVANTS of the people that ever lived. The world today needs the faithful servant — not the superior ruler. In Lincoln was fulfilled the words of Jesus who took upon himself the form of a servant."

Note now the

VI - SHOULDER PIECES.

The ephod was to have two shoulder pieces. *"It shall have the two shoulder pieces thereof joined at the two edges thereof: and so it shall be joined together"* (Exodus 28:7).

The shoulder pieces declare the truth of the strengthening and sustaining Christ. Strength we all need — for the sorrows of life. We often feel like praying the prayer the Psalmist prayed: *"O Lord, my strength, make haste to help me"* (Psalms 22:18). How good when we can, from experience say: *"The Lord is my strength"* (Hab. 3:19).

In Christ, we can go from strength to strength. In Christ, we can know how to be strong. We can sum up most of what the shoulder pieces signify in these words:

"Cast thy burden upon the Lord, and he shall sustain thee: he shall never suffer the righteous to be moved" (Psalms 55:22).

"Hast thou not known? Hast thou not heard, that the everlasting God, the Lord, the Creator of the ends of the earth, fainteth not, neither is weary? There is no searching of his understanding. He giveth power to the faint; and to them that have no might he increaseth strength. Even the youths shall faint and be weary, and the young men shall utterly fail: But they that wait upon the Lord shall renew their strength; they shall mount up with wings as eagles; they shall run, and not be weary; and they shall walk, and not faint" (Isa. 40:28-31).

"For I the Lord thy God will hold thy right hand, saying unto thee, Fear not, I will help thee. Fear not, thou worm Jacob, and ye men of Israel; I will help thee, saith the Lord and thy redeemer, the Holy One of Israel. Behold, I will make thee a new

*sharp threshing instrument having teeth: thou
shalt thresh the mountains, and beat them small
and shalt make the hills as chaff"* (Isa. 41:13-15).

*"Come unto me, all ye that labour and are heavy
laden, and I will give you rest"* (Matt. 11:28).

*"Casting all your care upon him; for he careth for
you"* (I Peter 5:7).

Consider now the

VII - MITRE

A mitre is mentioned as among the garments of glory
and beauty.
"A mitre" (Exodus 28:4).

*"And thou shalt make a plate of pure gold, and
grave upon it, like the engravings of a signet,
HOLINESS TO THE LORD. And thou shalt put it
on a blue lace, that it may be upon the mitre; upon
the forefront of the mitre it shall be"* (Exodus
28:36-37).

The mitre is emblematical of the OBEDIENT Christ.
The Bible speaks much of obedience. Christ, the great
Redeemer, gave perfect obedience to the will of his Father
— both in doing and in suffering, by the merit of which
sinners are justified. *"For as by one man's disobedience
many were made sinners, so by the obedience of one shall
many be made righteous"* (Romans 5:19).

The Book speaks of that voluntary, free, and cheerful
obedience which the angels in heaven yield to the commands of God. *"Bless the Lord, ye his angels, that excel in
strength, that do his commandments, hearkening unto the
voice of his word"* (Psalms 103:20).

The Bible speaks of that involuntary obedience which

devils and wicked men are forced to yield to the commands of God.

> *"And the Lord said unto Moses, Yet will I bring one plague more upon Pharaoh, and upon Egypt; afterwards he will let you go hence: when he shall let you go, he shall thrust you out hence altogether"* (Exodus 11:1).

"And the devil said unto him, ALL this power will I give thee, and the glory of them, for that is delivered unto me; and to whomsoever I will give it" (Luke 4:6).

The Bible speaks too, of the obedience of good men. *"I shall be obedient to his voice." "The obedient ear." "Obedient to the law." "The priests were obedient to the faith"* (Acts 6:7). *"To make Gentiles obedient by word and by deed." "Servants be obedient to your masters." "Children obey your parents." "They are contentious and do not obey the truth."*

Frank Crane writes:

"You have doubtless wondered at the marvellous rise and still more marvellous permanence of the Mohammedan faith. How a horde of half-naked barbarians poured out of the dry womb of Arabia, overturned the immemorial dynasties of the Orient, and almost extinguished the light of European civilization. The secret of their success is found in their own name for their religion; for they do not call it Mohammedanism, as we call our Christianity. They call it Islam; and as nearly as we can translate that untranslatable word it means 'It is the will of God!' For an ignorant savage who has learned how to obey will overthrow a false and faithless knight, though armed with brass and triple steel.

"Abraham was the founder of that race which has taught spirituality to the world, and which persists and keeps its blood true to a greater degree than any other stock. Why, according to Hebrew legend, was this man chosen? Among all the citizens of the earth, why was this man of Ur picked out by the eye of God as most worthy to be the 'father of the faithful'? Read the account of the sacrifice on Mount Moriah, and you will see. Abraham raises his hand to slay his son; he knows not why, only that he has been told by his friend and master, Jehovah. Then Jehovah cried: 'Stay thy hand! At last I have found one man who knows how to obey!' And in him, according to the prophecy, shall all the world be blessed.

"The noblest battle in history was that at Thermopylae where a handful of Greeks fought till they died against the swarming hordes of Persians. And the reason why it ranks as the supremest instance of patriotism is found in the inscription on the monument their countrymen set up there: 'Stranger, go and tell your people that we died having obeyed their words!"

But of all the great obediences known to history in all the ages there was no obedience like that of Jesus who came down from the heights of Deity to the depths of Humanity, down from the adorations of heaven to the abominations of earth, down from the adorations of heaven to the bruises of earth, down from the coronations of heaven to the curses of earth, down from the delights of heaven to the defamations of earth, down from the excellencies of heaven to the execrations of earth, down from the favor of the Father's face to the fury of wicked men's faces, down from the glory place to the gory place, down from the hallelujahs of heaven to the hisses of earth, down from the intercessions of heaven to the imprecations of men who hated him without a cause, down from the joys of heaven to the jeers of devilish accusers, down from the kindness of heaven to the killing of earth, down from the majesty of heaven to the miseries of earth, down from the notableness of heaven to the nothingness of earth, when He made Himself of "no reputation". down from the place of praise to the place of persecution, down from the rejoicing of heaven to the revilings of earth, down from the throne to the tree — the cross — where history of human guilt culminates.

How weighty the words Paul wrote the Phillipians:

"Who being in the form of God, thought it not robbery to be equal with God: But made himself of no reputation, and took upon him the form of a servant, and was made in the likeness of men: And being found in fashion as a man, he humbled himself, and became obedient unto death, even the death of the cross" (Phil. 2:6-8).

"To obey — for us — "is better than sacrifice," We should be obedient to all of God's commands.
"Thou shalt not lie."
"Thou shalt not commit adultery."
"Keep thyself pure."
"Bring the tithe to my house."
"Thou shalt not bear false witness."
Just as in obedience to the Cross was Jesus, so we should be to Christ.
Now — finally — consider

VIII - GOLDEN PLATE

"And thou shalt make a plate of pure gold, and grave upon it, like the engravings of a signet, HOLINESS TO THE LORD" (Exodus 28:36).

This symbolizes the HOLY Christ. Note these words:

"And of Levi he said, Let thy Thummim and thy Urim be with thy holy one, whom thou didst prove at Massah, and with whom thou didst strive at the waters of Meribah;" (Deut. 33:8).

"...unclean spirit...saying, Let us alone; what have we to do with thee, thou Jesus of Nazareth? Art thou come to destroy us? I know thee who thou art, the Holy One of God" (Mark 1:24).

"But ye denied the Holy One and the Just, and

desired a murderer to be granted unto you;" (Acts 3:14).

"But ye have an unction from the Holy One and ye know all things" (I John 2:20).

Thinking of how Aaron, dressed by Moses in garments of glory and beauty, was exalted and set apart from all the others, exalted above the people and yet for the people, we say that for two thousand years Jesus, whom God hath highly exalted and to whom God hath given a name which is above every name (Phil. 2) has been set forth in His aloneness upon the consciousness of the world.

The more Jesus is studied, analyzed, the more His character is taken apart, the more His life is submitted to critical analysis, each element of it, like the separate pieces in the garments of glory and beauty, the more it will reveal Christ to be the perfect, the glorious, the beautiful, the wonder of all wonders, perfect, man and very God — yea, the verity of God's truth, the beauty of God's holiness, the purity of God's nature, the surety of God's promise, the reality of God's love, the majesty of God's throne, the authority of God's power, the pity of God's heart, the legacy of God's will.